D1072140

Towards a Global Federalism

Towards a Global Federalism

William O. Douglas

*Associate Justice of
the Supreme Court of the United States*

New York • New York University Press
London • University of London Press Limited
1968

TX
3110
.D6
.T6

© 1968 by New York University
Library of Congress Catalog Card Number 68-31494
Manufactured in the United States of America

341
D737

To Cathy

DEC 8 1969

Contents

Foreword

The famous Jesuit, Nicolas Point, who was missionary to the Indians of Idaho and Montana in the first half of the last century, made the following observation:

> Any individual had the right to make war, even for the most trifling reason, and to make a war of extermination, mutilating, scalping, massacring women, children, and old people. Exploits of that nature were considered acts of courage. Such was the force of these customs, and of many others, that, among the savages, anyone who made the slightest attempt to abolish them would have been the most imprudent of men. Wilderness Kingdom (1967), p. 15.

That philosophy was an ancient one known to all the peoples of the world; it has a strong contemporary flavor; those who have dissented from the American policy in Vietnam might in fact think that the words "most imprudent of men" encompassed them. The so-called savage philosophy mentioned by Father Point was indeed reflected in Nasser's speech of May, 1967, closing Aquaba Gulf to Israeli ships.

Up to the forties there was limited damage that one demented or evil person could inflict on society by one act. Now one person could eliminate millions. It is now clear even to the optimist that we live in peril, with a constantly shrinking margin of error or miscalculation.

The President, in speaking of the modern reactor and its production of plutonium, spoke of their growing number around the world and said:

> . . . the secret diversion of even a small part of the plutonium they create could soon give every nation power to destroy civilization — if not life on this earth.

ix

A few scientists, notably Admiral Hyman Rickover, have sounded the alarm and sought to establish by law some safeguards against this galloping advance of technology. Many of these relate to the protection of individual claims and interests. Overriding all legal problems is the designing of legal remedies that will supplant the Regime of Force with a Rule of Law.

The right to wipe out a neighbor has been surrendered by every state that is part of a federal regime. The states agree to solve their differences by peaceful means and a federal government provides the machinery for resolving those disputes. We must seek that federal solution of international conflicts if we are to survive the atomic holocaust.

There are also some individual claims that must be recognized and honored at the federal level. The oppressed individual frequently has no remedy in his own capital. For like the American Negro he is often a prisoner of the system that rules him. It is beyond contradiction that if the American Negro where left to state law for his salvation, civil rights would be at a standstill in some areas. It was indeed independent federal courts applying federal law that ended the regime of segregation at the constitutional level. So far as relief by law is concerned, all of our minorities owe much of their progress to the federal regime. At the world level we must find instruments of law outside a particular nation that will release an individual from oppression. The search for that remedy is also a search for a new federalism.

The impoverished areas of the world must be brought into some kind of federal relation with the developed nations. The industrial powers have such command over the raw materials of the world and over the forces of technology that foreign aid has become almost a travesty. When the flow of brain power to them from the underdeveloped nations is added, the rich seem destined to get richer while the poor get poorer. The odds against the new nations are so great that they will never find security and opportunity for growth unless they have some federal axis for help and sustenance.

There is no all-inclusive body of international law to which reference can be made for solution of all those problems. As President Hussain of India recently said, while the roots of international law are deep, much must be fashioned anew to deal with modern electronic and jet-age problems, not merely with those of the age of sailing ships. And that law must be "based on the consent of all sections of the world community and be in line with the aspirations of humanity as a whole."

Our failure to face up to these four critical problems is a measure of the bankruptcy of my generation. Those over forty are the architects of the existing design; they are therefore largely impotent to deal with these problems. Their thinking has been warped and conditioned by one evil man (Stalin), by another who was ignorant of the world and its problems (Truman), and by a third (Churchill) who was a romanticist but a true apostle of the Rule of Force and white supremacy. These three men gave us the inheritance of the Cold War that has helped fill the world with suspicion and hate and made cooperative solutions of common problems extremely difficult.

As a result, my generation missed the opportunities to act creatively. The logic of its philosophy ended with the immensely wasteful and misspent effort in Vietnam. We did not see behind the facade of all the isms of the world and sense the powerful tides of nationalism and race that shape the events.

The foregoing is a brief account of the Stokes Lecture I gave at New York University in March, 1968.

My generation of Americans will mostly not understand this book. I write indeed for those under forty who now have the last clear chance to avoid Armageddon and to halt the wars between the Rich and the Poor, the Right and the Left, the Whites and the Colored.

WILLIAM O. DOUGLAS.

Towards a Global Federalism

Chapter I

Disputes Between Nations—
Law in Lieu of War

There is the common view, which George F. Kennan has stated in his *Memoirs,* that American foreign policy has suffered under regimes of legalists, that too much emphasis has been placed on treaties and international law, that pledges and promises in this field are only words on paper, that "covenants without the sword are but words." Kennan, steeped in the past, is symbolic of the political bankruptcy of my generation.

It was said, when our own Constitution was up for adoption or rejection, that the judicial branch was the weakest of the three because it had neither the sword nor control of the purse strings — two historic sources of power. The American judiciary has encountered many crises because of the lack of any such authority. It has, however, survived because of the consensus of our people to live under a Rule of Law. Particular decisions, particular judicial regimes have been disliked. But the Rule of Law has survived because it is the chosen way of life.

The Great Powers cannot perhaps be expected to reach a consensus that will quickly transform the world into a federation. But now is the time for summit meeting after summit meeting, whose agenda is composed of existing and potential conflicts and whose main emphasis is on procedures, such as arbitration or adjudication, which will be used in lieu of force for their solution.

Nations, like the men who compose them, are inherently predatory. Conflicts can never be eliminated. That is why the talk of "peace" is usually fradulent talk. The only talk that is constructive is how to design procedures to handle conflicts between nations. When we look ahead, we can say that those conflicts are as certain to develop as the sun is certain to rise.

1

The atomic age has greatly limited man's ability to cope with them in the conventional way. That is why the search for the Rule of Law is the most pressing problem of this century.

A Regime of Law, as contrasted to the Regime of Arms under which we now live, presents new, challenging problems that are at times irritating. On the domestic scene lawyers often "shop" around for a forum where the judge is apt to be friendly to their interests. I have heard these lawyers say, "I'd never trust a Communist judge." And I am sure his counterpart can be found in Communist lands.

One large question, of course, is the composition and nature of the tribunal or agency that will make the decision. Is it honest? Is it competent? Is it prejudiced?

Those problems confront every nation in providing tribunals for its internal controversies. We have had considerable experience at the world level both under the League of Nations and the United Nations in selecting judges for the International or World Court. Choosing those procedures that will safeguard the independence and competence of the tribunal are, of course, critically important, but in terms of planning and control they present a relatively simple problem to solve.

Mutual trust is a key ingredient of a Rule of Law. Henry L. Stimson, who was Secretary of War under Roosevelt and Truman, and who had a special responsibility in the development of the A-bomb, made an observation in March, 1946, which is extremely pertinent to our present problem:

> The chief lesson I have learned in a long life is that the only way to make a man trustworthy is to trust him; and the surest way to make him untrustworthy is to distrust him and show your distrust. And it is from this lesson that I draw the conviction that only a direct and open dealing with other nations on this, the most pressing problem of our time, can bring us enduring co-operation and an effective community of purpose among the nations of the earth. It is the first step on the path of unreserved co-operation among nations which is the most important. Once the course of national conviction and action is set in this direction by the example of the major powers of the world, petty differences will be recognized for what they are, and the way toward a real fraternity of nations will be open.

This is not to say that a nation must turn over a problem for the opposition to solve as it chooses. A "legal" question, as distinguished from a "political" one, has standards or guides to be employed and applied — precepts that have evolved as part of the general body of international law or that have been expressed in a treaty or convention. Moreover, a Rule of Law presupposes that the arbiters or judges will represent a cross section of the world community. No group — ideological, religious, or racial — must be made ineligible to sit. If it were, then the power structure that presently threatens to tear the world apart and reduce it to cinders would continue to operate under the guise of law. That would be intolerable.

There is no nation that does not have a tradition of law; we also know that the advocates and the jurists who are trained in the various systems are not venal. If I were to list the ten top legal scholars I have known, Russia, China, Japan, the Middle East, Africa, and Latin America would be included. The world does not yet have the same legal tradition at the level of international tribunals as we have at home. But the International Court of Justice has an admirable record. If one party or one protagonist always won — and there are some in this nation who think that is our manifest destiny — the tribunal that sits in judgment would not be worthy of the judicial tradition. The temptation is always great to manipulate an institution for one end or purpose. The Rule of Law is not founded on that premise.

There is a further consideration with which those who have an insular attitude are not familiar. Nationalism is a stronger force in the affairs of the world than communism, fascism, socialism, or free enterprise.

Vietnam is a good illustration. Part of this southern neighbor of China was long occupied by that country, independence being achieved by a war in the tenth century A.D. But after independence was won, Vietnam for another thousand years remained "tributary, in the Chinese cultural-political-psychological sense, taking China as a model" — to quote John K. Fairbank of Harvard. Vietnam has lived under the shadow of China from the beginning and will continue to do so and can never be expected to be a military base for operation against China. Yet being a complacent neighbor of China is far from being a puppet.

Nor is Vietnam a cradle of democracy. It is a land that has never known equal justice under law or other democratic principles. It has been nakedly totalitarian from time out of mind. It was in that tradition that Truong Dinh Dzu, who was the peace candidate coming in second in the presidential elections of 1967, was promptly placed under house arrest with no charges filed against him.

Corruption at various levels of government is also widespread. Even the president of South Vietnam, Nguyen Van Thieu, admitted (March 1, 1968) what everyone has known for a long time, that corruption in South Vietnam is a "serious disease." Thieu observed that this disease "has deep causes emerging from a national situation created by a century of foreign domination and twenty years of war marked by numerous political events."

China, Japan, France, and now the United States have dominated Vietnam. This domination reaches way back into the vitals of that nation, to the Chinese occupation.

The one overriding political reality in Southeast Asia is an anti-Chinese attitude. Chinese merchants came to contiguous North Vietnam as a result of trade and commerce and as a result of the thousand-year period of occupation of North Vietnam that ended A.D. 939. They went to the Philippines as merchants and traders. The Dutch invited them to Indonesia to make up a middle class of merchants. Many thousands came to Burma as refugees, crossing with ease the long, mountainous and largely unguarded frontier. The Chinese who settled in Malaya were brought there by the British — kidnapped off the docks of Canton at night and shipped out to that British colony to work in the tin mines.

American politicians like to picture these overseas Chinese as making up a network of spies and saboteurs for Peking. There doubtless are some among them. There can be no doubt that these overseas Chinese are a factor in Peking's reckoning. Peking has wanted to get remittances from them so that she can build up her currency reserves; and she has offered many rewards to residents of the mainland who receive overseas aid. The overseas nations have feared manipulation of their Chinese communities to do service for Peking.

Most of these overseas Chinese, however, are capitalists, not Communists. Indonesia before Sukarno's fall had a Communist Party of three million — the third largest in the world. But at least 85 per cent of them were Indonesians, not Chinese. Overseas Chinese, like overseas Americans, are proud of their motherland, whoever is in power. I suppose there was not a single overseas Chinese who was not thrilled when Peking's army almost drove the United Nations army from Korea. The reason was not exultation over communism but a sense of joy that China, long subdued and disgraced by the West, had at last become powerful.

Wherever the Chinese went (with the exception of Singapore), they ultimately prospered and in most of these places of which I speak they own an inordinate amount of the wealth. They are, in other words, the merchants, the capitalists, the financial element of each Southeast Asian country. This is due to the fact that they are not only able but extremely hardworking and aggressive — attributes that probably reflect their long evolution in the difficult, bitter climate of the northern regions of Asia. The Malay and other races in Southeast Asia are just as able but more easygoing. The environment in which they have long lived is not austere. Food, historically, has been plentiful. Since the rivers and oceans are filled with fish and the forests with an abundant supply of fruits, it has been easy to survive. So when the easygoing Malay lives for a few years in the same community with the hardworking Chinese, he discovers that he is working for a Chinese trucker or a Chinese restaurateur, fisherman, manufacturer, merchant, or banker.

This has given rise to deep-seated reaction against the Chinese similar in form to anti-Semitism. The result is often acts of violence. I remember a Chinese businessman being killed by a mob in Thailand when his building burned down allegedly because of a fire insurance policy. It was not difficult to predict in 1966 that when General Ky, head of South Vietnam, launched his anti-corruption drive, the first victim chosen for execution would be a Chinese, even though the prime grafters were the executioners.

This animosity is reflected in many discriminatory laws and practices. I once counted on the books of Thailand thirty-two different laws banning Chinese from various trades — one, for example, being the pushcart business, another being the carving of a statue of Buddha. This antipathy to the Chinese led to various efforts about ten years ago to eliminate all Chinese traders from the interior of Indonesia. This animosity is under the surface in the Philippines but still potent. The Philippines in 1954 adopted a retail trade act that bars aliens from engaging in retail trade and partnerships and corporations that are not wholly owned by Philippine citizens. This law, aimed at the Chinese merchant, had a grace period ending in 1964; but it has been strictly construed. Ownership of timber and mineral lands, and franchises to operate public utilities are restricted to citizens or business associations at least 60 per cent of whose members are citizens. A Chinese cannot purchase agricultural land nor even urban or residential land in the Philippines.

In Vietnam there are over 1,000,000 Chinese — 200,000 in the

North, 990,000 in the South, which is about 4 per cent of the total population. They own an inordinate percentage of the wealth; and in the minds of the Vietnamese, they represent a spectre of Peking domination.

When Nehru was visiting Ho Chi Minh in Hanoi in 1954, regarding the Geneva Conference, Ho Chi Minh asked: "How many Chinese do you have in India?" Nehru, puzzled, consulted with an aide and came up with the figure of 40,000. "Why do you ask?" Nehru inquired. "Because, you see, I have 500 million." This is why many believe that the greatest risk of Chinese domination of Vietnam is the presence of a foreign military expedition there.

It is said, of course, that Ho Chi Minh is a Communist who is the advance guard for Peking, Moscow, and international communism. He is Communist; but we know by now that the Communist world is not monolithic. Peking is on the extreme left and Yugoslavia and Outer Mongolia on the right. Whatever solidarity there may be regarding socialist philosophy, the export of the techniques of blood and thunder is no longer a common trait. Those of us who know Vietnam realize that the internal problems are stacked so high and the energies of the people so exhausted by twenty-five years of war that this little country would be unlikely to become a menace in Southeast Asia.

China of course is different, for she has not only a revolutionary mood but also atomic weapons. Yet China does not have the image of a world conqueror in the Western sense. China long had an empire; but it was unlike those of the European powers. China, to be sure, took over Tibet; but Nationalist Chinese and Communist Chinese alike believe that Tibet was historic Chinese territory. We of the West could present a powerful brief on the opposite side. Yet that Chinese conviction is deepseated.

The customary pattern has been for China to seek and receive tribute from nations as far south as Indonesia and as far north as Siberia. The nation, by paying tribute, was making obeisance to Peking and pledging itself against hostile actions. That pattern is deep in Chinese attitudes and still prevails. China seldom had an occupation army abroad. As John K. Fairbank recently said, that kind of empire means that "China has had little experience in dealing with equal allies or with a concert of equal powers and plural sovereignties."

She is big and powerful and, whether Communist or not, will have a vast zone of influence in Asia just as we do in the Americas.

On September 9, 1963, President Kennedy, when asked, "Mr. President have you had any reason to doubt this so-called 'domino theory,' that if South Viet-Nam falls, the rest of southeast Asia will go behind it?" answered: "No, I believe it. I believe it. I think that the struggle is close enough. China is so large, looms so high just beyond the frontiers, that if South Viet-Nam went, it would not only give them an improved geographic position for a guerrilla assault on Malaya, but would also give the impression that the wave of the future in Southeast Asia was China and the Communists. So I believe it."

William P. Bundy recently tied the struggle of the people of North Vietnam to the ambitions of Peking:

> . . . the nations of Southeast Asia are individually threatened by the parallel and naturally reinforcing ambitions of North Vietnam and of Communist China. A North Vietnamese take-over of the South by force would stimulate these expansionist ambitions and weaken the will and ability of the nations of Southeast Asia, and indeed beyond, to resist pressure and subversion."

But North Vietnam, struggling for independence from all foreign nations including China, hardly has the image of a Hitler bent on swallowing Southeast Asia.

Nor is China making war in Vietnam. The Vietnamese revolution is nationalistic under Communist leadership. Whether North Vietnam wins or loses, China will be untouched and as strong or as weak as ever.

Yet Secretary Rusk's October, 1967, analysis of the Vietnam situation makes it clear that the main strategy behind our Vietnam policy is to checkmate Peking.

> Within the next decade or two, there will be a billion Chinese on the mainland, armed with nuclear weapons, with no certainty about what their attitude toward the rest of Asia will be.
>
> Now the free nations of Asia will make up at least a billion people. They don't want China to overrun them on the basis of a doctrine of the world revolution. The militancy of China has isolated China, even within the Communist world, but they have not drawn back from it.
>
> Now we believe that the free nations of Asia must brace themselves, get themselves set; with secure, progressive, stable institutions of their own, with cooperation among the free nations of Asia — stretching from Korea and Japan right around to the subcontinent — if there is to be peace in Asia over the next 10 or 20 years. We would hope that in China there would emerge a generation of leadership that would

think seriously about what is called "peaceful co-existence," that would recognize the pragmatic necessity for human beings to live together in peace, rather than on a basis of continuing warfare.

Now from a strategic point of view, it is not very attractive to think of the world cut in two by Asian communism, reaching out through Southeast Asia and Indonesia, which we know has been their objective; and that these hundreds of millions of people in the free nations of Asia should be under the deadly and constant pressure of the authorities in Peking, so that their future is circumscribed by fear.

It is, however, the United States not China that has an expeditionary force in Vietnam. Peking, of course, supplies Hanoi with materials as we supply anti-Communists in the Dominican Republic with dollars and goods; and she has labor battalions there. China exists; she is in being — at least 700,000,000 strong. By the end of this century there will be as many Chinese in the world as there are people today. But as the New York Times says, if Rusk's statement is to be our policy, "de-escalation of American war aims will have to precede de-escalation of the war."

Something of a myth, however, is developing concerning the potency of our presence in Vietnam. President Eisenhower, in a Christmas statement in 1967, attributed to our troops in South Vietnam the collapse of the Communist ill-fated coup in Indonesia:

> Everybody knows that Sukarno was hand in glove with the Communist Chinese element in Peking. I am persuaded that without the presence of American forces in Vietnam the democratic leaders of the people of Indonesia might not have had the moral courage to clip his wings and tell him they were not about to turn their country into a Communist police state.

What Eisenhower overlooked was that the Communist attempt failed because the bullet intended for General Nasution only wounded him and he escaped over a wall in the dark and rallied the armed forces.

Peking is encouraging the poor areas of the world to arouse themselves and revolt. She offers some technical help and trains some cadres. But she is not sending military missions to lead guerrilla wars. In fact, she is telling the developing nations that they are on their own.

As Dr. Howard Schomer of the National Council of Churches recently said: "Although China, in isolation, anger, and inscrutable internal mystery, is not encouraging peace anywhere, yet she is not making war."

This was the gist of what Marshal Lin Piao said in September, 1965, when he promised "Mutual sympathy and support on the part of revolutionary peoples" — support that "serves precisely to help their self-reliant struggle."

A group of American scholars, headed by Edwin O. Reischauer, reviewed the Vietnam situation in December, 1967:

> At issue is the fate of many other peoples as well. It is not surprising that Peking and Hanoi have repeatedly proclaimed that this struggle has a direct meaning for the entire world. Can the technique of an externally aided "national liberation movement" as perfected by the Communists succeed in Vietnam? If so, future decisions inside as well as outside the international Communist movement will be strongly affected.
>
> To accept a Communist victory in Vietnam would serve as a major encouragement to those forces in the world opposing peaceful co-existence, to those elements committed to the thesis that violence is the best means of effecting change. It would gravely jeopardize the possibilities of a political equilibrium in Asia, seriously damage our credibility, deeply affect the morale — and the policies — of our Asian allies and the neutrals. These are not developments conducive to a long-range peace. They are more likely to prove precursors to larger, more costly wars.

The same fears were expressed by the Establishment when we had our revolution in 1776. Ideas are contagious, and the spectacle of long-pressed people breaking their bonds is both contagious and frightening.

This is no brief for Communist tactics. But it expresses one reaction to the feudal system that governs most of Southeast Asia. These feudal systems contain no regimes of law that allow orderly change. The *status quo* rides on the backs of the people in this benighted area. If there is to be a change for their betterment, it can come only by grace of the Establishment or by force and arms. The likelihood, therefore, is that there will be revolution after revolution in this troubled area, no matter what happens in Vietnam.

The moral is not that Regimes of Force are requisite solutions but rather that Regimes of Law are indispensable. In time there may be seizures of power by Communist Parties in parliamentary nations. But to date this has seldom happened, even in developing nations.

Our preoccupation with communism may promise to pull us into that vortex. We should, however, know by now that a military approach is not the answer. One does not need to be an expert to see that we have failed our military objective in Vietnam. As time passes, it seems that the cost and the effort have been so great as to discourage wars of national liberation elsewhere.

The price we have already paid in Vietnam should mean that future foreign forays into civil disorders will be discouraged. Edwin O. Reischauer who, as noted, suggested in December, 1967, that a Communist victory in Vietnam might well give credence to the domino theory, by the early part of 1968 had concluded that our Asian policy as implemented in Vietnam was a failure. Using as an analogy the flooding of an area by an adverse force, he concluded: "Asian states do not need military dikes so much as good economic land fill."

Any discussion of the way to displace a Regime of Force by a Rule of Law is certain to test each specific proposal against that international crisis which dominates the contemporary scene.

If the Great Powers had been dedicated to a Rule of Law rather than a Rule of Force, the much publicized Berlin issue could have gone to the International Court of Justice, or some other body, for settlement. The right of access to Berlin by the United States forces rests upon the construction of the Four-Power Agreements. There was nothing in the Agreements that ensured the right of access. But the question remains as to whether the many functions that the Four Powers had agreed to perform in Berlin fairly implied a right of access. This was the essence of the position of the United States as announced by Secretary of State George Marshall. It is that kind of problem which is grist for the judicial mill, because one of the functions of the most ancient of courts is the construction of contracts. This problem was ultimately resolved by diplomatic agreement. But meanwhile there had occurred one of the most dangerous confrontations which East and West had experienced. The failure to submit the issue to arbitration and adjudication certainly cannot be laid at the feet of the United States, since Secretary Marshall suggested it go to the Security Council. The result was a default by the Soviet Union. I mention it merely because it dramatizes one current and still dangerous issue susceptible of settlement by law without any show of arms.

Yesterday it was Berlin; today it is Vietnam. It will not do to say that if we, the people of the world, had been addicted to the Rule of Law, the present Vietnam situation would not have developed. Nor will it suffice to point out the mistakes that have been made.

While the whole background and antecedents of our present posture in Vietnam are relevant to an understanding of how a Rule of Law, as opposed to a Regime of Force, would operate at the very start of another such controversy, our initial question concerns the manner and method of using a Rule of Law to extricate ourselves from our present predicament and to stabilize the turbulence which the present contest had engendered.

In terms of a Rule of Law as applied to Vietnam, what do we do now?

In one of the many Senate debates on Vietnam during 1967, the following colloquy between Senator Dirksen and Senator Fulbright occurred:

> Mr. Dirksen: "What does the Senator want to do?"
> Mr. Fulbright: "I have said it."
> Mr. Dirksen: "Tell the Senate. Does the Senator want to quit now and pull out?"
> Mr. Fulbright: "What I would like to see happen — whether it will happen this way I do not know — is a reconvening of the Geneva Conference, and our agreeing to abide by the result. We did not agree the last time at the last minute. We refused to agree."
> Mr. Dirksen: "We were not even a signatory."

The Geneva Conference, held in 1954, was composed of representatives of the United Kingdom, the United States, the Soviet Union, France, Peking, Cambodia, Laos, Vietnam, and the Viet Minh regime. Partition was provided in an agreement of July 20, 1954. On July 21, 1954, a common declaration was issued by eight of the participants. The declaration of July 21 provided that the line of partition "should not in any way be interpreted as constituting a political or territorial boundary." Elections were to be held in July, 1956, "under the supervision of an international commission," looking toward a unification of the nation. And it was provided that "no military base at the disposition of a foreign state" should be established in either zone. The United States did not join the declaration but announced it would "refrain from the threat or the use of force to disturb" the agreement and would "view any renewal of the aggression . . . with grave concern and as seriously threatening international peace and security."

But it is uncontroverted that the United States used its power, prestige, and so-called moral leadership to make sure that the 1956 elections were not held. President Eisenhower announced that the election would have gone for Ho Chi Minh by a big majority. That would

certainly be true today; but in 1956 Ngo Dinh Diem was a great national figure and I thought then, and still think, that he would
have had a good chance of winning. But even if I am wrong and Eisenhower was right and the odds were in favor of Ho Chi Minh, there
certainly was nothing in the Geneva Accord that made the holding of
an election dependent on its outcome or that barred the people who
so chose from electing a Communist. A Communist head of Vietnam
would certainly be a different breed from a Communist head of China,
for the anti-Chinese attitude is very pervasive in that part of the
world. Moreover, as already noted, communism is not a monolithic
state — that it varies greatly as it evolves — with Peking on the far
left and countries like Yugoslavia and Outer Mongolia on the far
right. The significance of the free election clause in the Geneva Accord
was that it would have provided the mechanism for political change
and thereby would have brought an end to hostilities that have plagued
that little country for decades. But when there is no mechanism for
political change and the grievances pile high, force and arms will be
used in any country, just as they were used in this country in 1776.

The suggestion that the Vietnam crisis be referred to the Geneva
Conference contains all of the ingredients of a procedure pursuant
to a Rule of Law. First, it would invoke a multination tribunal that
would represent those nations with the most at stake in finding a solution to the problem. Second, the tribunal would have a background
of experience in the area and with the powerful tides that are running
there. Third, submission of the problem to the tribunal would be accompanied under the Fulbright proposal by an agreement to abide
by the decision. That would be a wholly different submission than
the one we chose for the Paris talks in the spring of 1968.

While Secretary Rusk has said that he too would like to see the Geneva Conference reconvened to address itself to the problems of Vietnam, he significantly failed to say that we would abide by the result.
But it is that consensus that is the essential ingredient of a Rule of
Law — the one feature distinguishing life under a legal regime from
life under a regime of unilateral action. Article 25 of the Charter of
the United Nations embodies that conception of consensus:

> The members of the United Nations agree to accept and carry out
> the decisions of the Security Council in accordance with the present
> charter.

A consensus is implicit in every legal system. It is the choice of law as opposed to force. In this atomic age the people of the world can afford no more delay in finding formulae for submitting disputes between nations to some court, committee, conference, or arbiter for decision.

The other crucial factor is agreement on the Rule of Law to be applied. The Geneva Conference of 1954 produced four basic principles to govern the situation: (1) a cessation of hostilities and a withdrawal of forces behind designated lines; (2) the eventual reintegration of the nation into one viable unit; (3) free national elections, appropriately supervised, to provide a national government representative of the wishes of all the Vietnamese people; and (4) the liquidation of all foreign military bases.

That frame of reference is at least a starting point both in terms of Vietnamese interests and of Asian stability.

I do not know Ho Chi Minh, and I have no direct contact with him. But I have received from him, through mutual friends, various communications. The most recent one came in March, 1968, about the time it was delivered to the Department of State. It dealt with the four main questions raised by Americans who do not trust Hanoi. It was indeed responsive to the President's statement at San Antonio, September 29, 1967:

> The United States is willing to stop all aerial and naval bombardment of North Vietnam when this will lead promptly to productive discussions. We, of course, assume that while discussions proceed, North Vietnam would not take advantage of the bombing cessation or limitation.

The message that Ho Chi Minh sent was as follows:

Q. If the bombing ceases, when will talks start?
A. 7 to 15 days.
Q. What will be the subject matter of the discussion?
A. Anything within the frame of reference of the Geneva Conference.
Q. Who will be parties to the talks?
A. North Viet Nam and the United States. Either can bring in another party.
Q. Will any advantage of the United States be taken in case of cessation of the bombing?
A. Hanoi accepts Clark Clifford's statement of January 25, 1968.

The position taken on that date by Secretary Clifford before the Senate Armed Services Committee was as follows:

> Senator Thurmond: "When you spoke of negotiating, in which case you would be willing to have a cessation of bombing, I presume you would contemplate that they would stop their military activities, too, in return for a cessation of bombing."
> Mr. Clifford: "No, that is not what I said.
> "I do not expect them to stop their military activities. I would expect to follow the language of the President when he said that if they would agree to start negotiations promptly and not take advantage of the pause in the bombing."
> Senator Thurmond: "What do you mean by taking advantage if they continue their military activities?"
> Mr. Clifford: "Their military activity will continue in South Vietnam, I assume, until there is a cease fire agreed upon. I assume that they will continue to transport the normal amount of goods, munitions, and men, to South Vietnam. I assume that we will continue to maintain our forces and support our forces during that period. So what I am suggesting, in the language of the President is, that he would insist that they not take advantage of the suspension of the bombing."

It was in response to that message from Ho Chi Minh that the President on March 31, 1968 (when he announced he would not be a candidate for reelection), talked about a possible peace in Vietnam saying, "Peace can be based on the Geneva Accords of 1954." But, as noted, the formula used in the Paris talks following that announcement was quite a different breed than the one hopefully promised.

There are other ways of settling the Vietnam controversy pursuant to a Rule of Law.

Resort to the Security Council or to the General Assembly is an alternative.

Article 33 of the United Nations Charter provides:

> 1. The parties to any dispute, the continuance of which is likely to endanger the maintenance of international peace and security, shall, first of all, seek a solution by negotiation, enquiry, mediation, conciliation, arbitration, judicial settlement, resort to regional agencies or arrangements, or other peaceful means of their own choice.
> 2. The Security Council shall, when it deems necessary, call upon the parties to settle their dispute by such means.

Article 37 provides that if the parties fail to settle an Article 33 dispute, "they shall refer it to the Security Council."

By Article 39, the Security Council "shall determine the existence of any threat to the peace, breach of the peace, or act of aggression" and make recommendations or decide what measures shall be taken to maintain or restore "international peace and security."

The "regional agencies" referred to in Article 33 are also sanctioned by Article 52, which permits such agencies to do the necessary policing. Yet Article 53 provides that no regional enforcement action shall be taken without the authorization of the Security Council.

Ambassador Goldberg has stated that "certain members" of the Security Council, presumably the Soviet Union and France, have kept the Vietnam issue from the Council's agenda. On the other hand, unofficial sources have indicated that the United States has not presented the problem to the Council because of private warnings that a resolution calling for halting the bombing of North Vietnam would be introduced and that many of the Council members would vote for such a resolution, thus requiring an American or Nationalist Chinese veto. In any event, the failure of the Security Council to consider the question does not preclude effective UN debate and possible action. In accordance with the Uniting for Peace Resolution of 1950, which the United States vigorously supported during the Korean War days, we could well submit the issue to the General Assembly for its consideration. That Resolution provides:

> If the Security Council, because of lack of unanimity of the permanent members, fails to exercise its primary responsibility for the maintenance of international peace and security in any case where there appears to be a threat to the peace, breach of the peace, or act of aggression, the General Assembly shall consider the matter immediately with a view to making appropriate recommendations to Members for collective measures, including in the case of a breach of the peace or act of aggression, the use of armed force when necessary, to maintain or restore international peace and security.

In short, the collective action envisaged by the Charter precludes unilateral action no matter how righteous the intervening nation may feel about its action.

The Vietcong is equally unwilling to submit to the Rule of Law of the Charter. The obligation to take the matter to the Security Council is not conditioned on one's judgment as to what he thinks the Security Council might or might not do. A commitment to a Rule of Law excludes such lawlessness.

Still another alternative, which has been proposed in at least one bill in Congress, would be to refer the Vietnam controversy to the International Court of Justice. It is a justiciable — as distinguished from a political — issue since it involves construction of the Geneva Accord of 1954, the United Nations Charter, and various treaties.

The United States, in accepting the general jurisdiction of the International Court of Justice, pursuant to Article 36 (2) of the Court's statute, declined to submit "disputes with regards to matters which are essentially within the domestic jurisdiction of the United States of America *as determined by the United States of America.*"

This is the so-called Connally Amendment, which in practical effect means that the United States will not agree to submit to the jurisdiction of the Court unless in each case it gives explicit approval.

The Statute of the Court provides that the Court decides only controversies between states; and it prescribes that those decisions shall be decided "in accordance with international law." And it is specifically provided that in the event "of a dispute as to whether the Court has jurisdiction, the matter shall be settled by the decision of the Court." The Senate Committee in its report on the Connally Amendment stated:

> A provision similar in principle is found in article 2, paragraph 7, of the Charter, providing that nothing in the Charter shall authorize the organization to intervene in essentially domestic matters. The committee feels that the principle is also implicit in the nature of international law, which, under article 38, paragraph 1, of the statute, it is the duty of the Court to apply. International law is, by definition, the body of rights and duties governing states in their relations with each other and does not, therefore, concern itself with matters of domestic jurisdiction. The question of what is properly a matter of international law is, in case of dispute, appropriate for decision by the Court itself, since, if it were left to the decision of each individual state, it would be possible to withhold any case from adjudication on the plea that it is a matter of domestic jurisdiction.
>
> It was also brought to the attention of the subcommittee that a number of states, in filing declarations under the statute of the Permanent Court of International Justice, interposed reservations similar to that of the resolution under consideration, but in no case did they reserve to themselves the right of decision. The committee therefore decided that a reservation of the right of decision as to what are matters essentially within domestic jurisdiction would tend to defeat the purposes which it is hoped to achieve by means of the proposed declaration. . . .

But the matter was otherwise resolved, as I have said, although in the *Interhandel Case* four Justices of the International Court of Justice expressed the view that our reservation was ineffective.

Both President Eisenhower and President Kennedy tried to eliminate the critical words in the Connally Amendment that paralyzed any usefulness of the International Court — not the reservation of disputes "essentially within the domestic jurisdiction of the United States" but the words that immediately follow *"as determined by the United States of America."* Senators Humphrey, Morse, and Javits were active in this regard. They argued that as a world power we should help develop, at the world level, institutions "which will give a sense of stability and organization to the world community." But they failed.

The Connally Amendment also includes disputes under a multilateral treaty, unless all the parties are before the Court and unless the United States especially agrees to its jurisdiction.

It has become quite common, however, for the United States in multilateral treaties to accept jurisdiction of the International Court for disputes arising under those conventions. As of 1966, some twenty multilateral treaties make such a provision, though in seventeen other conventions covering economic cooperation and aid agreements provisions for the referral of disputes to the International Court of Justice are subject to the self-judging domestic jurisdiction reservation of the United States.

These submissions to the jurisdiction of the International Court are made pursuant to Article 36, paragraph 1 of the Court's statute. They are not based on the general jurisdiction provisions of Art. 36, par. 2.

Resort to the Court pursuant to the latter section has been clouded by many reservations which have been made respecting its jurisdiction.

As of 1967, Liberia, Mexico, South Africa, and the Sudan had declarations substantially similar to that of the United States, as expressed in the Connally Amendment.

States in the British Commonwealth commonly reserve disputes with member nations in the Commonwealth.

Others, some eleven in number, make exceptions for disputes with regard to questions which by international law fall exclusively within the jurisdiction of the particular state. But unlike the U. S. they do not reserve the right to determine for themselves which disputes are encompassed by this exception. And then there are some twenty-three states that have filed declarations in which there are no substantive limitations of any consequence imposed on their acceptance of the jurisdiction of the Court.

A nation that may not be sued without its consent will not, as a matter of reciprocity, be able to sue another nation if the latter objects. The result is that the use of the Court has become so infrequent and the number of cases coming before it for lack of jurisdiction has dropped to such low numbers that as of 1967 only a minority of the member nations of the UN had filed any declaration concerning acceptance of the jurisdiction of the Court.

The position of the Soviet Union is similar to that of the United States, namely, that the jurisdiction of the International Court should be voluntary and not compulsory, and it has even opposed the use of the General Assembly of the International Court of Justice for advisory opinions.

In view of our resistance to the International Court, an agreement by the United States to submit the Vietnam issue to it would have a worldwide electrifying effect.

The International Court of Justice is an integral part of a world regime of law. But it is not by any means the exclusive one. When we envisage a Rule of Law we do not infer that the world will be run by judges. There are many other peaceful means for solving disputes between nations.

Hardly a day passes without *diplomatic negotiations* producing a settlement of some difference, great or small, between nations. Treaties are one product of diplomacy; executive agreements, another. But less formal agreements that quiet disputes or solve them are legion.

The *good offices* of a third party is another procedure in a Regime of Law — a device that usually fulfills its function when the opposed parties are induced to resume direct negotiations.

Mediation is a closely related procedure, the mediator seeking to reconcile opposing claims and find an acceptable solution without fanfare or publicity and usually without any report.

Commissions of Inquiry are often used to help resolve issues of fact after an impartial investigation. They report on the issues of fact, usually without recommendations.

Conciliation Commissions may investigate the facts and recommend a settlement to the parties. Here again there is no element of compulsion behind the report, only a hope that there will be a friendly settlement. Related to the Conciliation Commissions are the procedures of the UN and OAS in supplying to member states lists of qualified persons to serve on commissions of inquiry and conciliation.

Arbitration and/or *Judicial Adjudication* provide a full-blown Rule of Law. First, the decisions are made on the basis of legal principles or precedents. The Hague Conventions state that disputes should be adjudicated "on the basis of respect for law"; the International Court of Justice by Article 38 of its Statute provides for settlement on the basis of international conventions, international custom and the general principles of law "recognized by civilized nations." Second, the decision rendered is binding on the parties.

Not every international dispute, however, raises a "legal" question. Some are "political" in the sense that their settlement involves reference to standards or considerations not crystallized as yet into "law." The purposes of the United Nations as stated in Article I of the Charter are not only to promote settlements of disputes "in conformity with the principles of justice and international law" but also to prevent and remove "threats to the peace" and to suppress "acts of aggression or other breaches of the peace."

The procedures for peaceful settlement of international disputes — whether "legal" or "political" — are as numerous and as versatile as the needs require. In the case of "legal" disputes, a vast body of law and precedents exists. Though standards may not be adequate to cover an oncoming dispute, new guidelines can be provided.

Though man's inventive genius in law is as great as his skill in science, he is greatly in default when it comes to the major issues that fill the world with alarm at the prospect of atomic war.

The legal adviser of the State Department, Leonard C. Meeker, calls those who are opposed to unilateral action as distinguished from a Rule of Law, the "fundamentalists." His contention is that unilateral intervention in Vietnam and in the Dominican Republic reflects "the world which law is trying to shape." But the law that is made unilaterally is the law of a bygone day. Self-defense, as for example against the installation of missiles in Cuba, is justified. By the same token, the Soviet Union had the right to protest American missiles in Turkey. But apart from self-defense, unilateral action has no justification. The freewheeling concept of making law fit one's idea of the shape of the world to be can be used by any great power.

If we of the West can take unto ourselves the power to put down a civil war promoting a "hostile" ideology, Russia has the same prerogatives, and in time so will China.

If we can take unilateral action to defeat "communism" in Vietnam, Russia can marshal the forces to liquidate "democracy" in Israel. The spectre of a properous dynamic Israel is as disturbing to any Communist regime as the possibility of a Communist takeover in Vietnam is to us.

The world is headed for great revolutionary convulsions. It is not a choice between revolution and evolution, but a choice between peaceful revolution and violent revolution. At times the yoke on the back of the people is religious, at times military, at times feudal, and these three often combine. Two Maryknoll Fathers, Thomas R. Melville and Arthur Melville, and a nun, Marion P. Bradford, working in Guatemala recently brought this whole problem to the surface.

They described the three rightwing groups in Guatemala that during the last eighteen months have assassinated more than 2,800 intellectuals, students, labor leaders, and peasants "who have in any way tried to organize and combat the ills of Guatemala Society." Of those killed, "not more than one in ten" is "probably a communist."

They shot a man who was trying to organize a union on a sugar plantation. Men forming cooperatives were shot. The oligarchy, composed of the landowners and the army, will go to any lengths to prevent the peasant from acquiring "any real economic or political power."

The peasant works "now for 80 cents a day while the rich make and bank millions from his sweat. He will be allowed to improve if it's simply a question of putting in toilets or digging wells, but anything that would alter the oligarchy's life-and-death control over him will be resisted with the worst of viciousness."

The alternatives are submission or rebellion, and the indications are that the peasants will not submit much longer. These two priests conclude:

> Having come to the conclusion that the actual state of violence, composed of the malnutrition, ignorance, sickness and hunger of the vast majority of the Guatemalan population, is the direct result of a capitalistic system that makes the defenseless Indian compete against the powerful and well-armed landowner, my brother and I decided not to be silent accomplices of the mass murder that this system generates.

We began teaching the Indians that no one will defend their rights, if they do not defend them themselves. If the government and oligarchy are using arms to maintain them in their position of misery, then they have the obligation to take up arms and defend their God-given right to be men.

Accordingly, they cooperated with groups that were sending supplies and other aid to guerrilla forces and, if the reports are correct, had some associations with pro-Castro agents. Their reply was: "When the fight breaks out more in the open, let the world know that we do it not for Russia, not for China, nor for any other country, but for Guatemala. Our response to the present situation is not because we have read either Marx or Lenin, but because we have read the New Testament."

Thomas Melville and Marion Bradford (now his wife) have disclosed that they will form a "Christian front" to cooperate with guerrilla movements. Their activities and that of other "reformist" clergy have triggered a fresh look by the Latin Church into its role in Latin America. The church is sharply split between conservative forces and voices of reform. This question of reform in the Latin Church is not limited to one country, but pervades all of the nations of the South, excepting of course, Cuba. The church, traditionally a unifying and powerful force in Latin America, can become by its own example, a leader in political and economic reform. On the other hand, preservation of the *status quo* by an unflinching hierarchical structure, with its monopoly over Latin American religious life, can only lead to political, economic, and religious disaster.

The miserable and desperate condition of most of the people of the world promises revolution after revolution. Some of them will be Communist; all of them will be suspect as Communist inspired. How many will the United States seek to put down? We are told by an Assistant Secretary of Defense:

The United States has now deployed the equivalent of about eight divisions and their supporting units to Vietnam. . . . this has been done without mobilization of Reserve Forces. As those eight divisions have been deployed, however, we have added to the active forces the equivalent of three divisions plus their support units and we have added to the Priority Reserve two divisions plus their support units. Thus, despite the tremendous build-up in Southeast Asia involving the equivalent of eight divisions and supporting units, five of these eight have, in effect, been replaced here at home. This fact becomes evident in another manner by comparing the actual strength figures. The 353,000 who made up the active Strategic Reserve in June, 1965, have been reduced only to 303,000. The 411,000 in the Priority Reserve Forces have been increased to 520,000, and the readiness of their units increased. The nation thus now has active land forces available for deployment capability that are only 14 percent less than before the Southeast Asia build-up, while our Priority Reserve Forces have been increased by 24 percent.

All of these forces can be deployed, fully equipped, while we continue to support our forces now in Vietnam. We do not, therefore, see the basis for [the] suggestion that the United States might not be able to cope with a second major conflict.

In 1967, the Senate Armed Services Committee disapproved the construction of a new class of fast deployment logistics ships. They would be deployed throughout the world near troubled spots. Our troops would be flown there in case of uprisings. The Committee said:

> Beyond the cost, the committee is concerned about the possible creation of an impression that the United States has assumed the function of policing the world and that it can be thought to be at least considering intervention in any kind of strife or commotion occurring in any of the nations of the world. Moreover, if our involvement in foreign conflicts can be made quicker and easier, there is the temptation to intervene in many situations.

The temptation of the Great Powers is strong to intervene in revolutionary situations close to their borders, e.g., Russia in Iran, the United States in Mexico. Equally strong is a temptation to intervene in revolutionary situations where the country beset is a vast potential supplier of raw material for the industrial plants of the Great Powers. Brunei and Indonesia of Southeast Asia are examples. The Congo of Africa is another. If unilateral action is the pattern of the future, it seems almost certain that Armageddon is our ultimate fate.

We are raised in the tradition that our security rests on a balance of power. Britain ruled the waves and kept a troubled world under control. Now the role has passed to us. If there were no atomic bomb, if there were no powerful competing ideologies, if the entire world were not in revolt against poverty, illiteracy, and misgovernment, American unilateral action might be successful. But world conditions have so greatly changed that unilateral action is practice in the art of brinkmanship.

The "Dog of War," to use a Jeffersonian expression, usually takes on a religious cast. Like the Crusades, the cause seems to be holy and righteous, the opposition representing the forces of evil. The Cold War has conditioned us to that mood. Everything Communist is suspect; everything Communist is evil; every utterance of a Communist spokesman has ulterior motives. "No one can trust the Russians" has become an article of faith.

No one can trust any nation where a course of action runs against its self-interest or imperils its existence. Owen Lattimore, our foremost China expert, tells us that the only way to understand that nation is to take the perspective, Inside China Looking Out. If we viewed a particular nation from the perspective with which that nation sees the world, we would have a greater understanding of the forces that propel it and condition its thinking. This does not mean that conflicts and disputes would be ended. They would, however, be greatly limited. Certainly every people wants survival; and as that is more and more jeopardized, the chances of reaching a consensus that ensures survival should be greater.

There are powerful people in Washington, D. C., who would now drop "the bomb" on the Chinese mainland, liquidating in a few minutes its nuclear and industrial power.

"What happens when they rebuild and gain once more their nuclear and industrial position?"

"That would take five years. Then we could bomb them again."

That alternative — the opposite of a Rule of Law — is frightening and appalling. For it reintroduces America in the awful role it played at Hiroshima. We become, in other words, the modern Genghis Khan.

A recent article in the Soviet *Literary Gazette* charges Mao Tsetung with a plan to set up "a sort of super state embracing not only Eastern and Central, but later even Western, Asia." That article says that the strategy is to generate "a global atomic conflict." It adds, "That is why it [Peking] continues year after year doing everything to increase international tension and pour oil on fire wherever it breaks out in the world."

Our first step toward realization of a Rule of Law for world affairs starts with Peking, now a virtual outlaw in the community of nations.

Pope John in his famous Pacem-in-Terris urged discourse and dialogue between the Communist world and the rest of us:

> Meetings and agreements in the various sectors of daily life, be-
> tween believers and those who do not believe or believe insufficiently
> because they adhere to error, can be occasions for discovering truth
> and paying homage to it.

The discourse is the beginning not the end.

How can we lend a hand in making a viable world that includes
Peking? By bringing Peking into the United Nations. John K. Fairbank has stated:

> The Communist capacity for impeding orderly procedures, ob-
> structing and sabotaging collective effort, is well known. The prospect
> of getting mainland China into the international organization is not
> one to gladden the heart of any official who must deal with the result-
> ing situation. No one should assume that our China problem will be
> easier. The argument for getting Peking in is simply one of choice
> between evils. The trouble it brings will be less grievous than the war-
> fare that seems likely if Sino-American relations remain on their
> present track. We have learned to prefer small limited wars to big
> nuclear disasters. So we should try to substitute diplomatic wrangling
> and nasty competition with China all across the board in place of a
> prolonged military showdown.
> In short, Peking's presence in the UN is no panacea nor is it likely
> to seem to be a great improvement. It may at first seem like a disaster,
> and this has deterred every administration in Washington. But the
> presence of China in the UN offers a prospect of diversifying the
> struggle and diverting it from the military single track.

This is not an easy path. For the dialogue with Peking that may
resolve the major differences is likely to be long and exhausting. It
may wear out the negotiators. But the desire to survive is common
ground we have with all peoples, the immediate problem being to
find the formulae that will divert disputes and controversies into
channels that lead away from the atomic holocaust. I use the word
divert rather than avoid because man is basically predatory and emotional.

The legal tools for establishing a Rule of Law are treaties and
conventions. Through these devices the United States and Russia
have been busy dealing with aspects of the atomic age. We made a
treaty with Russia to ban nuclear tests. A "hot line" was established
between the White House and the Kremlin by executive agreement.
Nuclear weapons were barred from outer space by a 1967 treaty with
many nations. A treaty on the non-proliferation of nuclear weapons

was submitted to the UN Disarmament Conference at Geneva in January, 1968, which has sent a draft to the General Assembly. But cooperation between the two countries extends far beyond this one aspect. Despite ideological differences, we have concluded over forty treaties and executive agreements with Soviet Russia since 1917, including agreements on commerce, cultural relations, lend-lease, telecommunications, visas, aviation, desalination, fisheries' judicial procedure, prisoners of war, and the rights of neutrals at sea. Of these, twenty-five are still in force today.

Treaties and conventions are as old as civilization. Usually they formulate a rule of law for the disputants. Those generated by the United Nations and its specialized agencies are not legion, but they are more than four hundred. They touch on a wide variety of subjects — arbitration, banning of obscene literature, protection of broadcasters, prevention of genocide, suppression of traffic in women, children, and slaves, promotion of political rights of women, control of narcotics, tariffs agreements, peaceful use of outer space, resources of the high seas, the foot and mouth disease, carriage by air, equality of treatment under compensation acts of national and foreign workers, underground work of women in mines, child labor at sea, collective bargaining, safety of life at sea, telegraph, telephone, and radio regulations, copyrights, and dozens of other conventions touching a myriad of subjects.

Some of these conventions pertain to disputes between nations. Others deal only with commitments to bring internal laws up to certain standards. Some create international agencies to deal with common problems. One such is the International Atomic Energy Agency organized "to accelerate and enlarge the contribution of atomic energy to peace, health and prosperity throughout the world."

The Single Convention on Narcotic Drugs 1961, ratified by the United States in 1967, designates international control organs to perform the functions for the parties, those organs to be paid by the United Nations. The scheme is, in substance, an embryonic, world government in this single, select field with ultimate jurisdiction over disputes vested in the International Court of Justice.

The Telecommunication Convention of November 12, 1965, to which 121 nations had subscribed at the start of 1967, eases those methods of communication and makes possible the accommodation of numerous conflicting interests. The Postal Union gives a nation the right of its people to send letters to some 130 nations and to receive letters from these nations. The Convention on Civil Aviation is greatly responsible for the efficient network of air routes over some 90 nations around the globe.

The Convention on Fishing and Conservation of the Living Resources of the High Seas was ratified by some 20 nations and effective in 1966. Basically it is an international conservation measure designed to secure a maximum supply of food and other marine products from the ocean. Disputes arising under it shall at the request of any party either be submitted to a special commission of five members or sought to be resolved under Article 33. If a commission is used, the parties will select the members, failing which they shall be named by the Secretary General of the UN. There is a special provision that any state that is a party may name one of its nationals to the commission with the right to full participation "but without the right to vote or to take part in the writing of the commission's decision." Standards to guide the commission are provided, among which are:

— That scientific findings demonstrate the necessity of conservation measures;
— That the specific measures are based on scientific findings and are practicable; and
— That the measures do not discriminate, in form or in fact, against fishermen of other States.

And provision is made that the decision of the commission will be binding on the states concerned.

Thus we have in this troublesome field of fisheries, where feelings often run high and tensions dangerously mount, the start of a regime of law. The idea is not to send destroyers or planes against greedy fishermen of other nations, but to resort to law.

Yet the Soviets do not like the obligatory settlement provisions, so they have not joined. Nor has Japan. Nor have coastal states who do not like to give up control over their adjacent waters. The result is that the signatory nations represent only 15 per cent of the annual take from the oceans. At the same time, fishing practices are putting greater pressure on the fish resources, threatening depletion as the population mounts. The world is ready in a scientific and technical sense for full controls. Immaturity exists at the political level. Yet the fisheries problem illustrates, according to the experts, that no nation can much longer proceed unilaterally.

A further step forward was made on November 25, 1967, when by Executive Agreement, the United States and the Soviet Union agreed to collaborate in fishery research and to protect red hake and silver hake in designated portions of the Atlantic. The protection takes the form of abstaining from fishing during certain months and not increasing the fish catch above the 1967 level in certain waters. Other restrictions were agreed upon relative to scup and fluke; and waters to which fishing vessels of the Soviet Union have access were described.

These treaties in general achieve four things:

— They create international agencies to carry on activities of mutual concern to all or to many nations.

— They provide ground rules for carrying on various international activities.

— They endeavor to induce or encourage nations to adopt guarantees of human rights hitherto lacking in many areas.

— And, as we shall see, they provide at times a machinery and procedure that will resolve disputes between the signatory nations.

The United Nations is roundly criticized as an ineffective agency in resolving international disputes. The Charter requires all states to refrain from the use of force in international affairs except in defense or pursuant to certain collective arrangements. The Charter requires all states to settle their controversies by peaceful measures. Intervening in the internal affairs of another nation is disapproved. Yet most nations have sought excuses for not working under the Charter when it comes to vital issues. Once an excuse is sought, it usually can be found. Since the UN seems unable to settle the major controversies, whether they involve Hungary or Goa, Vietnam, Rhodesia, or the Egyptian-Israeli conflict, people rush to the conclusion that it is utterly ineffective. In spite of these minus aspects, the UN does provide a meeting place for argument and debate. It brings together all of the contestants both in informal and in formal session, and perhaps its greatest services are rendered at the informal level where people do meet and talk and where there are measurable advances toward solutions even though they are not recorded on television or related on the radio or expounded in the press.

Beyond all that is the work of its specialized agencies. The four hundred-odd treaties they have inspired have helped round out the great mosaic of international law that now touches the lives of people everywhere. These treaties theoretically dilute the sovereignty of every participating nation. But in truth each signatory uses its sovereignty to acquire benefits for its people that otherwise would be lacking. Just as residents of a community through joint action can have health protection, security against criminals, beauty through zoning, and the like, so can members of the international community use their sovereignties to help the world become a viable society.

Such cooperation is essential to begin the task of resolving the great and irrevocable differences in the world. Communism versus the free society represents one conflict. Kashmir poses the question whether a nation should be established solely on religious lines. Other conflicts between nations have racial overtones.

The manifest destiny of one nation, whether due to feelings of insecurity or whether based on economic interests or others reflecting ideological differences, often seems utterly opposed to the manifest destiny of another nation. Yet in this atomic age compromises within livable limits are necessary. The main need is to develop conciliation, mediation, and adjudication as part of the specific functions of the UN. The problem is not whether the UN's decisions can be enforced, it is whether the conference table rather than troop movements is to be used and whether at the conference table the matter can be settled or passed on to some other agency or tribunal for compromise or adjudication.

Our *Dred Scott* decision was not honored and a bloody Civil War followed. But most of our judicial decisions — state and federal — are honored without show of force. The reason is that our people have decided that they will try to live under court decisions whether they like them or not.

It is that kind of consensus at the international level which we must seek and find, if we are to survive the atomic holocaust.

As already noted, Article 33 of the United Nations Charter demands that parties to any dispute, "the continuance of which is likely to endanger the maintenance of international peace and security," shall resort to "peaceful means" of settlement.

The United Nations Charter condemns "acts of aggression or other breaches of the peace" (Art. 1, § 1), and it imposes on all members the duty to settle peacefully "international disputes or situations which might lead to a breach of the peace" (Art. 1, § 1). The terms aggressive war and breach of the peace are not defined; and many scholars and diplomats have spent days, weeks, and months seeking definitions. The problem is so complicated that at this juncture an effort at universal codification is probably not possible. Aggression is outlawed but self-defense is permitted. If a mechanistic definition were adopted, a nation that first moved its troops across a border would be branded the aggressor. Yet the provocation of a neighbor might be so ominous that the nation threatened might perish unless it moved first. As the late Chief Justice Stone said in reference to the Nuremberg Trials, "The idea of the aggressor is so vague and uncertain that a law punishing those who wage aggressive war will be a weapon by the victor against the vanquished." Many international conferences have been held in an effort to find a satisfactory legal definition of the term "aggression." The League of Nations first considered it in 1924. It has been repeatedly considered by agencies of the United Nations well into the 1960's. No agreement has yet been reached. In time perhaps there will be an agreement, though I suspect it will be only illustrative, not definitive. The same is true of breach of the peace, a concept familiar to all regimes of domestic law. In the United States it is often used as an excuse for suppressing an unpopular minority or to put an end to the exposition of unpopular views. The dangers of unscrupulous use at the international level are equally as great.

I do not suggest abandoning the precepts of the Charter. Rather, I suggest a more modest start. Let us ask, *What are the kinds of disputes that historically and in our time have endangered international peace? Which of them are already so related to existing principles of international law that their adjudication by arbiters, agencies, commissions, tribunals, or courts is customary and not revolutionary?* I put the matter that way because the problem is to find a consensus. A consensus can be reached only if the Great Powers lead the way. The search for common ground between them is therefore the starting point.

Territorial Issues

I start with a Russian proposal that was transmitted by Khrushchev in a note to all heads of state or governments on January 3, 1964. The main theme of this note was to propose an end to the use of "force for the settlement of territorial issues." In this proposal he reviewed the interests of European nations, African nations, and Latin American nations in putting an end to forceful settlement of territorial claims.

He correctly stated, "A peaceful settlement of territorial disputes is . . . favored by the fact that in the practice of international relations there already exists a store of improved methods of peaceful settlement of outstanding issues." He proposed "an international agreement or treaty on the renunciation by states of the use of force for the solution of territorial disputes on questions of frontiers." The heart of his recommendation was his proposal that there be "an undertaking to settle all territorial disputes exclusively by peaceful means, such as negotiation, mediation, conciliatory procedure and also other peaceful means at the choice of the parties concerned in accordance with the Charter of the United Nations."

President Johnson's reply to Mr. Khrushchev agreed with the Russian proposal in principle, and stated that the United States was prepared to propose guidelines even "broader and stronger." These guidelines suggested by the President were as follows:

> *First,* all governments or regimes shall abstain from the direct or indirect threat or use of force to change:
>
> — international boundaries;
> — other territorial or administrative demarcation or dividing lines established or confirmed by international agreement or practice;
> — the dispositions of truce or military armistice agreements; or
> — arrangements or procedures concerning access to, passage across or the administration of those areas where international agreement or practice has established or confirmed such arrangements or procedures.
>
> Nor shall any government or regime use or threaten force to enlarge the territory under its control or administration by overthrowing or displacing established authorities.
>
> *Second,* these limitations shall apply regardless of the direct or indirect form which such threat or use of force might take, whether in the form of aggression, subversion, or clandestine supply of arms; regardless of what justification or purpose is advanced; and regardless of any question of recognition, diplomatic relations, or differences of political systems.
>
> *Third,* the parties to any serious dispute, in adhering to these principles, shall seek a solution by peaceful means — resorting to negotiation, mediation, conciliation, arbitration, judicial settlement, action by a regional or appropriate United Nations agency or other peaceful means of their own choice.

Fourth, these obligations, if they are to continue, would have to be quite generally observed. Any departure would require reappraisal; and the inherent right of self-defense which is recognized in Article 51 of the United Nations Charter would, in any event, remain fully operative.

But what happened to the summit meetings, the only devices that could make these proposals a living reality?

President Johnson on October 7, 1966, opposed the use of force to resolve "territorial and border disputes" in Europe, saying that was "the bedrock" of our foreign policy. It should also be our policy in Southeast Asia and in the Middle East and in all other regions where new or ancient quarrels break out with shows of violence.

Boundary questions, one type of territorial dispute, are sometimes handled by tribunals chosen by the contesting nations. Such was the case of the Indo-Pakistan dispute over the boundary in the area of Rann of Kutch. A tribunal, Gunnar Lagergren, Chairman, was constituted pursuant to the agreement of June 30, 1965, and its award giving 10 per cent of the contested area to Pakistan was recently accepted by India. Our quarrel over the American-Canadian border in the Straits of San Juan De Fuca was resolved in 1872 by the Emperor of Germany pursuant to an article in the Treaty of Washington of 1871. Our controversy with Canada over the Alaska boundary was settled in 1903 by a tribunal of "six impartial jurists of repute, who shall consider judicially the questions submitted to them" — three being nominees of the King, three, of the President. In 1967, India and Burma agreed on a Commission to settle the various questions concerning their eight hundred-mile boundary. Other like examples are numerous though not legion.

Boundary questions are of course grist for the mill of the International Court of Justice. In 1959 it resolved such an issue between Belgium and the Netherlands. In 1962 it resolved one between Thailand and Cambodia.

Disputes over territory, apart from boundary controversies, are also familiar to that Court. In 1953 it resolved an issue between France and the United Kingdom concerning sovereignty over the islets and rocks of the Erebos and Minquiers groups. In 1960 the Court held that in 1954 Portugal had a right of passage over certain Indian territory, in respect of private persons, civil officials, and goods in general (but not in respect of armed forces, armed police, or arms and ammunition), to the extent necessary, as claimed by Portugal, for the exercise of its sovereignty over certain enclaves, and subject to the regulation and control of India.

A consensus to submit territorial issues to the processes of adjudication would route the Arab complaints against Israel away from military ventures. An Arab scholar recently stated the Arab position:

> It must be understood that the Arabs do not recognize Israel. Israel is the only state in the world which has no legal boundaries except the natural one the Mediterranean provides. The rest are nothing more than armistice lines, can never be continued as political or territorial boundaries. The presence of Israel on the Gulf of Aqaba is therefore not recognized at all by the Arab States.

Whether a nation has a legal existence and boundaries is certainly ripe for settlement by international law.

Use of Territorial and International Waters

The second Rule of Law with respect to which the great powers should seek a consensus is by no means original with the Soviets, but it was suggested by them as long ago as 1933. The Soviet proposal read:

> 1. The aggressor in an international conflict shall be considered that State which is the first to take any of the following actions:

> •   •   •   •   •

> (e) The establishment of a naval blockade of the coast or ports of another State.

This idea originally was adumbrated when the League of Nations in its disarmament conferences was beginning to try to distinguish between offensive armament and defensive armament, and sought in that connection a definition of an "aggressor." The aggressor as defined by the Soviets included the nation which was the first to take any number of various actions, the only one with which I am now concerned being "the establishment of a naval blockade of the coasts or ports of another state." I would remove the proposal from the setting in which it originated and suggest broadly that all questions pertaining to the use of international waters and territorial waters by any nation be submitted to some form of adjudication. The importance of this was illustrated recently by Nassar's statement, "The Aqaba Gulf constitutes our Egyptian territorial waters. Under no circumstances will we allow the Israeli flag to pass through the Aqaba Gulf."

The territorial sea is that portion of waters adjacent to the coast of a state over which the state exercises sovereignty pursuant to principles of international law. International waterways include for our purposes international straits and rivers and interoceanic canals.

The traditional extent of the territorial sea was three nautical miles. This limit, however, is not generally accepted at present, and the tendency is to claim a greater area, such as six or twelve miles, or in the case of certain Latin American countries two hundred miles. The issue — a continuously troublesome one as evident from the seizure of American fishing boats within two hundred miles of Ecuador and Peru — has been one of the major topics of discussion at international conferences.

Once the jurisdictional extent of the territorial sea has been determined, the further problem arises as to how to measure the limit in cases of highly irregular coastlines. These two issues, that have often arisen in connection with assertions of fishing rights, may also be relevant to disputes over oil and other wealth beneath the ocean. Such disputes may be resolved by treaty or diplomatic discussion; or they may even find their way into an international court, such as occurred in the *Fisheries Case* in 1951. There the International Court of Justice conceded Norwegian claims to sovereignty over a certain portion of contiguous sea out to a four-mile limit. The proper method of measurement was neatly at issue because of the erratic Norwegian coastline.

Other disputes concerning the territorial sea arise from a clash of interests between the nation exercising sovereignty over the area and nations whose ships must enter or pass through the waters. Customary international law subjects vessels entering the territorial waters of another nation to the jurisdiction of the sovereign state. Treaty stipulations may, of course, modify this principle. And customary international law has itself developed two exceptions to the rule: the right of "innocent passage" of foreign vessels through territorial waters, and the guarantee of immunity to a vessel that has entered the waters in distress. Disputes have arisen when the sovereign state has sought to apply its laws to vessels within its waters; and defenses based on "innocent passage," or entry in distress, or treaty provi-

sions have been asserted. It is common for such disputes to be resolved by arbitral panels or commissions or courts.

International controversies respecting international straits and rivers and interoceanic canals present a somewhat different aspect of the
problem. International rights in relation to straits and rivers depend
largely on international usage and practice, as noted, for example, in
the famous *Corfu Channel Case* of 1949. With respect to interoceanic
canals — of which there are three (Suez, Panama, and Kiel) — rights
of nations arise by dedication of the canal to international use.

The types of disputes which arise with respect to international
waterways are varied. One is the extent to which foreign vessels are
entitled to the free use of the waterway, a problem for which there
may be a different answer in time of peace or war. A related concern is the right of a riparian nation to exercise reasonable regulatory
powers over the waterway, and its corresponding duty to ensure safe
navigation for ships using the waterway.

In the case of interoceanic canals, the amount to be charged for
tolls or the proper currency for payment may provoke a dispute.
The interests of the operating authority and user states, although generally in agreement respecting maximum use of the waterway, may
well conflict on those issues. In addition to its customs and sanitary
regulations, the territorial sovereign will seek to exercise control over
crimes committed in its territorial waters and over entry of persons,
and to guarantee its own security.

A related problem, whose explosive nature has been neatly outlined by the North Korean seizure of the Pueblo, is the jurisdiction
which a coastal state may exercise over vessels not within its territorial
waters, but upon the high seas in an area contiguous to those waters.
International law has analogized jurisdiction over activities within
territorial waters to those within the land boundaries of a state. Outside territorial waters, however, the question of jurisdiction becomes a
bit muddied. Although there have been occasional statements to the
effect that jurisdiction over the high seas is concurrent, shared by all
nations equally, the better and generally accepted view is that within
a certain part of the high seas adjacent to the territorial water line,
the coastal state possesses "preventive" or "protective" jurisdiction to
secure enforcement of its laws or the defense of its shores.

The problem then arises, of course, which laws may be enforced
in adjacent waters and what is the limit of self-defense?

Our own experience offers some useful examples of preventive jurisdiction. Since 1790, the United States has asserted jurisdiction up to a twelve-mile limit for enforcement of its customs laws. Moreover, during the days of the Eighteenth Amendment, the United States often seized ships, particularly British vessels, which hovered outside the three-mile limit but sent liquor in to the mainland by launching small craft. And our 1935 Anti-Smuggling Act permits the President under specific circumstances to proclaim a "customs-enforcement area" up to sixty-two miles from shore. Enforcement of quarantine, immigration, and sanitation measures are also common examples, both in this country and around the world.

A state's attempt to enforce its laws outside of its territorial waters has often led to countries facing one another in trying circumstances. One outstanding example is the explosive situation caused by Russian seizure of American sealing vessels in the 1890's. The ships and crews were seized beyond Russian territorial waters, and were hauled into Vladivostok or Petropavlovska. Some sailors were denied shelter from hunger and cold, and their captain was obliged to secure lodging for them in a shed; others were subjected to harsh and unjust treatment. Despite the dangerous situation, the two countries managed to settle their differences in 1902 by peaceful arbitration, which resulted in compensation being awarded to the United States. Another confrontation, this time between Great Britain and the United States, arose from American seizure of British vessels, outside the three-mile limit, that were engaged in smuggling liquor into the United States contrary to the National Prohibition Act. After a number of seizures, and a warning by the British that continuance of the practice would be regarded as creating "a very serious situation," the two countries began negotiations that eventually led to a treaty governing the boarding and seizure of vessels beyond the three-mile limit.

Regarding protective jurisdiction for purposes of self-defense, the practice of nations is less uniform, and not at all clear. In the famous *Virginius* case, a ship bound ostensibly for Costa Rica was in reality transporting men and arms to aid insurgent activities in Cuba in the year 1870. A Spanish warship seized her on the high seas. Many of those on board were summarily tried and executed after the ship had been brought in to a Cuban port. During World War I, the United States, while still neutral, protested against British cruisers patrolling the waters close to American shores but beyond the three-mile limit. Again, during World War I, several nations proclaimed neutral zones extending beyond territorial waters, and asserted the right to police them for the security of the country. And in 1939, the American states issued the Declaration of Panama, in which they declared:

> As a measure of continental self-protection, the American republics, so long as they maintain their neutrality, are as of inherent right entitled to have those waters adjacent to the American Continent, which they regard as of primary concern and direct utility in their relations, free from the commission of any hostile act by any non-American belligerent nation, whether such hostile act be attempted or made from land, sea, or air.

The adjacent waters were defined by lines extending into the Pacific and Atlantic Oceans, at some points several hundred miles out. Collective or individual patrolling by American states was permitted in "the waters adjacent to their coasts within the area above defined." The Declaration was characterized by the United States, however, as "merely a statement of principle, based on the inherent right of self-protection rather than a formal proposal for the modification of international law." And those European nations engaged in hostilities took the position that the Declaration was not binding upon them without their consent.

Perhaps the best statement of international practice regarding protective jurisdiction in adjacent waters was offered by Phillip Jessup in 1927, when he observed:

> . . . the conclusion may be drawn that there is a tendency on the part of many states to claim in the interests of self-protection, a certain power of control over the high seas adjacent to territorial waters. It is obvious that this tendency is not universal and no general principle of international law may be deduced therefrom. It is merely possible to say that reasonable claims advanced on the ground of self-defense, particularly in time of war, are logically sound and legally defensible.

This "rule of reasonableness" approach parallels the observation of Chief Justice Marshall in *Church* v. *Hubbart,* 2 Cranch 187. The Chief Justice noted with respect to laws passed by a state to secure itself from injury and enforced beyond the limits of the territorial sea that "[i]f they are such as unnecessarily to vex and harass lawful foreign commerce, foreign nations will resist their exercise. If they are such as are reasonable and necessary to secure their laws from violation, they will be submitted to."

Jessup took a like view concerning preventive jurisdiction, saying:

> There seems, however to be sufficient evidence of acquiescence in
> reasonable claims to warrant the assertion that a customary rule of
> international law has grown up under which such acts may be held
> legal if they meet the test of reasonableness. The relative vagueness of
> this norm makes it necessary to state that a nation acts in such cases
> at its peril, its definitive vindication depending upon ultimate deter-
> mination by some international tribunal. In the present stage of
> international development it is impossible to be dogmatic concerning
> general categories of acts.

Jessup's observations remain valid today, although efforts have
been made to codify rules for national jurisdiction over areas of the
high seas. For example, in 1929 the Harvard Research in International Law proposed a rule providing that "The navigation of the
high sea is free to all states. On the high sea adjacent to the marginal
sea, however, a state may take such measures as may be necessary for
the enforcement within its territory or territorial waters of its customs,
navigation, sanitary or police laws or regulations, or for its immediate
protection." The 1958 Geneva Conference on the Law of the Sea
adopted Article 24 of the Convention on the Territorial Sea and the
Contiguous Zone, providing that

> 1. In a zone of the high seas contiguous to its territorial sea, the
> coastal State may exercise the control necessary to:
> (a) Prevent infringement of its customs, fiscal, immigration or sani-
>   tary regulations within its territory or territorial sea;
> (b) Punish infringement of the above regulations committed within
>   its territory or territorial sea.
> 2. The contiguous zone may not extend beyond twelve miles from
> the baseline from which the breadth of the territorial sea is measured.

It should be noted that even though the Geneva Convention limits
the contiguous zone to twelve miles from the coastline, there exists
in international law a more general protective jurisdiction principle
permitting a state to reach and punish conduct outside its territory
that endangers its security or impairs its governmental functions.
Two common examples are the counterfeiting of one state's currency
in another country, or perjury by an alien immigrant before a consular
official located in the alien's country. The types of conduct considered
to threaten the security of a state have not, however, been clearly es-

tablished. Counterfeiting and falsifying official documents come within the general class. The American Law Institute, in its Second Restatement of the Foreign Relations Law of the United States, recognized the absence of controlling rules, and suggested that the class should be limited to conduct "generally recognized as a crime under the law of states that have reasonably developed legal systems."

There is also the principle of "hot pursuit," approved by the 1958 Geneva Conference, permitting the ships of a coastal state to pursue continuously a vessel outside of territorial waters if the latter has committed an offense and the chase has begun within those waters.

I submit that even these fulminant problems of national jurisdiction over portions of the high seas contiguous to territorial waters are ripe for judicial settlement. Although some have argued that the questions raised are properly for the political branches of government to solve, the more common view is to treat the matter as a legal problem. Courts have long dealt with various aspects of these questions, the outstanding judicial cases in this country being those involving enforcement of the National Prohibition Act. The issues, moreover, are appropriate for judicial review. Although the answers are not cut and dried, the guidelines are discoverable in the body of international law. At the same time, we are bound to see — as in the case of the *Pueblo* — probings for a diplomatic solution. Although legal standards are discoverable, they are yet debatable. The interests of the offended state in what it envisions as its security or as the necessary enforcement of its laws are often drawn in emotional terms; in these circumstances, submission of the controversy to an international tribunal may well seem impractical if not impossible. Yet these disputes that threaten our very existence must find some means of resolution beyond diplomatic ploys and probings. A common interest of mankind in survival offers the most significant hope for channeling these disputes into some international tribunal for decision — whether that be an international court, an arbitral panel, the UN, or a regional body.

The development of customary international law as a standard to settle disputes concerning international waterways has been hindered by the fact that the status of international waterways has generally been established and controlled by treaties or conventions. At the same time, drafters of agreements tend to draw from other treaties and conventions already in force covering similar problems, so that a type of customary-treaty law has developed. In addition, useful analogies exist in other areas of customary international law that can be used to resolve disputes — a method employed, for example, by the Permanent Court on International Justice in the *S. S. Wimbledon Case.* A 1959 survey among independent states indicates that co-riparian nations have entered into formal agreements (covering a very high proportion of the world's international waterways) for compulsory adjudication or other third-party settlements of disputes.

In short, in the case of international and territorial waters, disputes and methods of resolving them are numerous. The Pueblo incident involving the United States and North Korea and the Aqaba Gulf incident involving Egypt and Israel are recent inflammatory examples. A representative listing of common disputes would include, in addition to those already noted: detentions of neutral vessels and seizures of enemy cargoes; collisions between ships; water boundaries; and the jurisdiction of an international agency charged with the supervision and maintenance of a waterway. Methods or resolution are just as varied: international conferences and reports by committees of international organizations; acts of an international organization or discussions within the organization among the parties affected; treaties or conventions; special international conferences called to deal with specific problems, such as the two London conferences held to discuss solutions to the 1956 Suez crisis; simple diplomatic discussions; cooperation by two nations each with its own regulatory agency; representation of interested nations on commissions controlling the waterways; use of national courts applying principles of international law; submission to arbitral panels or mixed claims commissions; and submission to the jurisdiction of an international court. With regard to the two latter methods it should be noted that arbitral tribunals and international courts possess the advantage of a tribunal composed of impartial judges, though commonly the states involved in the dispute have judges of their own nationality sitting on the tribunal.

Nations have generally been able to find peaceful solutions to problems concerning international and territorial waters, although, as always, there are exceptions, one being the Egyptian-Israeli dispute over the Suez Canal and Straits of Tiran, which to this day remains unsettled despite both peaceful and hostile efforts.

If there is the will, there is now a way for a Rule of Law to take the place of a regime of force in settling all disputes over international waterways and territorial waters.

If the Great Powers reached a consensus that all territorial issues,

including boundaries, and all questions pertaining to the use of terri-
torial and international waterways would be settled by mediation, ar-
bitration, or adjudication, we would be well on our way to establish-
ing a Rule of Law governing the major controversies. If the Great
Powers agreed, the other nations would be bound to follow, for no
small adventurer would dare flout these basic tenets of the new world
order.

The Ocean Floor

Although freedom of the high seas has been a principle of international law for a substantial period of time, expanding technology
is presently threatening even that entrenched rule. The principle was
developed to regulate the activities of man as he sailed the oceans,
but there are no laws to govern man in his exploration and use of
undersea phenomena beyond the extent of a state's territorial sea and
continental shelf. Soon man will be capable of working at any depth
in the oceans, and the treasures in the waters — marine life, vegeta-
tion, mineral deposits — will be there to seize.

In December, 1967, the UN General Assembly, in response to a
proposal submitted by Malta in August, 1967, established an *ad hoc*
committee composed of representatives from various member states
to examine the question of reserving for exclusively peaceful purposes the seabed and the ocean floor, including the subsoil, underly-
ing the high seas beyond the limits of present national jurisdiction.
The study committee was directed to analyze the scientific, technical, economic, legal, and other aspects of the problem, and to suggest
practical means of promoting international cooperation in the exploration, conservation, and use of the riches of the ocean floor.

In March, 1968, this Special Committee opened meetings on the
peaceful exploration and development of the ocean floor. A report
will probably be available when the General Assembly reconvenes
late in 1968.

The Maltese proposal in effect called for the internationalization
of the ocean floor, and recommended an international framework
for the use and economic exploitation of resources. There was some
predictable adverse reaction in Congress following the introduction
of the Maltese proposal. The United States, however, was one of the
forty nations sponsoring the December, 1967, General Assembly
resolution establishing a study committee. Britain was also a sponsor,
as was Japan, though Russia was not.

Various proposals were recently made by Senator Pell of Rhode Island to model a treaty for ocean space after the new treaty on outer space. Under his most recent proposal (March 5, 1968) the exploration and exploitation of the seabeds by each nation that is a party to the treaty would be done "only under licenses issued by a licensing authority" designated by the United Nations. The Maltese proposal is different; under it, the high seas and the floor beneath would be "a common heritage of mankind," belonging to all nations but to none. Under the Maltese proposal the exportation of the wealth of the ocean floor would be used to aid the development of the world's poorer countries.

Any treaty containing the Pell proposal would, of course, have to prescribe claims of national sovereignty over the ocean floor. The nature and extent of the continental shelf would also have to be explicitly defined. An international authority would be established to coordinate exploration and development of the ocean floor by governmental and private research bodies.

Under the Maltese proposal, there would also be an international authority with more pervasive powers necessary for sharing the wealth of the ocean floor with all nations.

The conclusion and ratification of the treaty on outer space offers significant hope that man can also reach agreement on the peaceful exploration and use of the vast undersea areas of our world before emerging technology leads to chaos.

The Maltese proposal would not only forestall a race by the developed nations to appropriate for themselves the bulk of the riches of the ocean floor; it is a challenging proposal that would in effect create a new global federalism founded on the necessity of managing a common resource for the benefit of all nations of the world. The ocean floor would indeed become the force binding the world into a new indissoluble union, first for exploiting the wealth of the ocean, and, beyond that, for managing the universal concerns of men.

It is the Maltese proposal that we should promote with all our vigor.

Conclusion

Those categories — territorial questions; disputes involving international and territorial waters; and the ocean floor — would by no means exhaust the questions that endanger the peace of the world.

But they embrace an important segment. In time, others could be added.

The creation by the General Assembly of a standing committee or committees on conciliation and mediation would be helpful. In the days ahead there will be a series of disruptive problems which may be more "political" than "legal" and which will require quick attention. The Congo is of a different species than Vietnam; Cyprus is still another; the Arab plan to exterminate Israel, as well as many others that will arise, are *sui generis*. Standing committees of the General Assembly would be ready to move instantly; and in the long run they might be able to distill from recurring controversies new principles that could be expressed in terms of international law in the same fashion as the four hundred-odd UN conventions already mentioned.

Our greatest current plague is the persistence of the Cold War. We had no monopoly in its creation; but we have exploited it so extensively that everything about "communism" has an evil cast. Yet when the anatomy of that system is exposed, say at the level of medicare, scientific research and development, athletics and the arts, technical training, nursery schools, outer space, the regime obviously reflects much that is good from the viewpoint of all humanity.

The Communist system once was monolithic with a dominant Stalinistic cast; and that led to our "containment" policy. But as Alf M. Landon recently observed, the monolithic nature of communism has changed. Its fragmentation makes United States policy "outmoded." "Building bridges" with Communist nations is the prime necessity of the day.

We have heard much about coexistence, very little about coevolution. Coexistence in the sense of maintenance of the *status quo* in the world is impossible. Societies change, their entire character being transformed by time and events. We pride ourselves on free enterprise. Yet American business is greatly dependent on government largesse. Without Pentagon contracts — or like subsidies — there would be great pockets of depression. We have, in other words, moved from free enterprise to a *sui generis* form of socialism. The trend toward the collective society will continue, for we now know that no matter the growth rate of our GNP, the private sector will not be able to take care of employment needs. Technological advances are so great that disemployment will mark our future. In other words the public sector and government *largesse* will be the mainstay of most of our people.

Communist countries also are experiencing evolutionary change. The private sector is increasing, though not at the same tempo as our public sector.

In sum, the Western and the Soviet regimes may yet evolve into comparable economic systems.

Beyond that is the messianic zeal which propels these competing ideologies. There is a religious fervor in their promotion. Each is backed by zealous prophets. Each has its own dynamism, its relentless drive for world acceptance. Neither can be long contained. Ideas are contagious and enduring. If all the books on Marxism and Leninism were burned, their ideas would endure and people in some lands would still march to the measure of their thoughts. The same is true of the ideas of Madison, Jefferson, and Lincoln.

A world regime founded on law would have to accommodate these competing schools of thought. It could not presume to cope with civil disorder say in Hungary that sought to establish a free society or in Brazil where revolutionaries desired to establish communism.

The new federalism would deal with conflicts between nations just as our own Supreme Court deals with conflicts between sovereign states. Internal disorder would be beyond its competence, save and unless that disorder spilled over into a neighboring state. Precedent is not lacking. I have already mentioned various agreements between the United States and Soviet Russia designed to deal with a wide variety of problems.

As this is being written, we read of orbital weapons to deliver the bomb and of over-the-horizon radar to detect their trajectory. These new weapons systems were apparently designed originally to devastate vulnerable missile sites. But as the missile bases have been dug deeper into the ground and their protection increased, the new systems have become essentially mass-kill weapons that can rain unimaginable destruction on cities and civilians.

Our over-the-horizon radar system was designed primarily to counteract the Russian FOBS, or Fractional Orbital Bombardment System. A vehicle is sent into a fractional orbit containing large-yield nuclear weapons, perhaps significantly larger than one hundred megatons. These could be exploded at a high altitude (50 to 150 miles above earth), igniting fierce fires over a wide ground area. The

Russian system would not violate the recent space treaty, for FOBS would not place nuclear weapons in a full orbit around the earth. Even though over-the-horizon radar — which in simple terms uses the earth's ionosphere as a mirror — could detect FOBS launchings, detection is not foolproof, for the mirror could be clouded if Russia detonated a large-yield device over her own territory, say in Siberia.

The United States, true to the philosophy of the arms war, has developed its own delivery technique called MIRV, or Multiple Independently Targeted Re-entry Vehicle. MIRV consists essentially of a cluster of nuclear bombs on a single missile, which can drop them off upon previously designated targets.

These new children of technology have been born in the historic pattern of "preparedness" that has always resulted in war. It proves that while we are enlightened in science, we still live in the Stone Age when it comes to emotions.

Reciprocal sanity means there should be competition of a different sort. What proposals for a Rule of Law would improve relations between all men and guarantee, as opposed to a Regime of Force, escape from the horrors of nuclear war?

I once fought in a war that was waged to end all wars. I was so innocent I believed that that could and would be the result. Now I know that one war only lays the foundation for the next one — because the victor imposes too severe penalties on the loser or because the loser must have revenge or because the dislocations caused by the conflict inspire new and collateral uprisings or revolts. That endless cycle is no longer tolerable, because all humanity will be in the crucible once the nuclear war starts.

If the instinct for preservation is not powerful enough, the appeal to the pocketbook may be. When will people realize that war with arms produced by modern technology is much, much too expensive ever to wage?

Chapter II

Human Rights at the International Level

In his January 6, 1941 message to Congress, Roosevelt talked about "a world founded upon four essential human freedoms":

Freedom of speech and expression,
Freedom to worship God in his own way everywhere in the world,
Freedom of want,
Freedom from fear — "which, translated into world terms, means a world-wide reduction of armaments to such a point and in in such a thorough fashion that no nation will be in a position to commit an act of physical aggression against any neighbor — anywhere in the world."

"Freedom," he said, "means the supremacy of human rights everywhere."

The world interest in human rights is old and sustained. Hitler's *Mein Kampf* had a catalytic effect and aroused people as never before over national blueprints for human destruction.

Only one country in the world today admits practicing slavery; but it exists in about thirty countries. It is estimated that there are between 2,000,000 and 4,000,000 slaves in the world as of 1967. Africa supplies the greatest number through kidnaping, through sales by a family of one or more of its members, through subjugation of one tribe by a stronger one. A strong male slave today sells for $600 in Africa, a price which mounts as the human chattel reaches the principal market in the Middle East. It is estimated that the brothels of the Middle East are filled mostly with female slaves.

When under Hitler arbitrary detention and murder became the order of the day, leading jurists and lawyers of the world responded with various proposals. The idea was to make law supreme by fashioning procedures and creating tribunals capable of acting at the international level.

We have seen throughout history genocide in operation. The 6,000,000 Jews who were sacrificed in Europe head the modern list. Next probably come the Armenians who suffered the same fate some forty years ago at the hands of the Turks. But the practice persists and is continuing to this day. The most recent chapter has been written in Indonesia where up to 1,000,000 so-called "communists," many of them Chinese, have been liquidated. This vast liquidation has gone on with hardly a single voice of the West being raised in protest. There was no tribunal to which the victims could appeal. The only possibility of reaching public opinion was through the mass media, and they were generally not sympathetic with those charged with being "communist."

The much publicized Ayub, dictator of Pakistan, has let untrained military officers try civil and criminal cases, even though Pakistan is blessed with much legal and judicial talent.

In Turkey it is a brand-new crime to import any literature in the Kurdish language.

In Iraq there is equality for most Arabs but little for the Kurds.

The Shah of Iran freely uses military courts to try civilians, contrary to the Iranian Constitution. Bamian Ghashghai, a student in California, returned to Teheran to obtain financial help to continue his studies here. He was arrested, charged with inciting revolution, tried by a military court, and immediately shot. There should be at least a regional court to which such a person could resort for relief.

The recent military take-over in Greece has resulted in thousands being imprisoned or detained, not for criminal acts but for dangerous libertarian thoughts or ideas. They have no remedy at home and none at the international level.

The new federalism will in time have to deal with some aspects of human rights. This is a problem of great perplexities and of vast dimensions. It means bringing the nations of the world into a more intimate, working relation than has ever yet been possible. Its greatest obstacle is that for many people a Rule of Law is either remote or not an immediate concern. Some indeed have never known a Rule of Law in the Western sense of the term.

Hungry men must, of course, eat before they make ringing declarations of freedom of speech.

They must have good health and protection from pestilence before they can fully enjoy religious liberty.

They must have civic education and a degree of literacy before they can formulate safeguards against police practices.

They must be politically alive before they can deal with the problems of arbitrary use of power.

Yet a Rule of Law is necessary before freedom of speech, religious liberty, protection against oppressive police practices, and a guarantee of other civil rights is possible. They do not flourish where rights are subject to the whim or caprice of the powers-that-be.

Even those nations that have known a Rule of Law, experienced it under a colonial regime where many laws had a bias against the "native." The result was that many came to distrust law and took as their duty the evasion of it rather than respect and obedience.

Russia has a commitment to a part of the extensive bundle of human rights, the right to counsel in criminal cases being one, free education, equal rights for women, medical care, and the right to vote being others.

Most written constitutions have glowing affirmations of human rights. A prime example is the proposed Constitution for Ghana, drafted by a special Constitutional Commission established following the February, 1966, overthrow of the government, which was presented to the National Liberation Council in early 1968. The document can be numbered among the most far-reaching as respects guaranteeing an extensive array of political and individual rights. But in Africa, Asia, Latin America, and the Middle East these covenants often have little living meaning. Since World War II and the emergence of the new nations, many promising constitutions have indeed been torn up: Indonesia (1959), South Vietnam (1963), Thailand (1958), Pakistan (1958), Burma (1962) (*de facto*), Iran (1953), Greece (1967). The Dominican Republic is an example in this hemisphere (1964).

Though a constitution still exists, a military regime has often made its declaration of human rights a pronouncement of empty phrases.

China — and areas dominated by her — have never professed a dedication to a Rule of Law. That attitude long antedated the rise of communism. Hsun Tsu in the third century B.C. wrote:

There is a ruling man but not a ruling regulation . . . Law cannot stand alone and regulation cannot be exercised by itself. By getting the (right) man, it lasts; by losing the (right) man, it perishes. Law is the tip of government, and the great man is the source of governing. Therefore by having the great man (in control) although the law is incomplete, it will be sufficient to cover everything. Without a great man, even if the law is complete, the sequence of its application will be in disorder and will be unable to meet the change of events, and will lead to disorder.

The Confucian principles evolving from this creed were many, including (a) the unification of the judicial and legislative functions, i.e., the nonexistence of an independent judiciary; and (b) the virtual nonexistence of a legal profession. This Confucian attitude is largely reflected in the Chinese Communist approach to law. It is also reflected in Korea and Vietnam — wherever the mandarin tradition has put down its roots.

The full flowering of human rights at the world level may therefore be in the millennium.

Yet the ferment for recognition and enforcement of human rights is a powerful force around the world; and the United Nations gave expression to its appeal when it ratified the Universal Declaration of Human Rights in 1948.

Many of the rights enumerated in the Declaration reflect the philosophy of the modern welfare state — the right to social security (Art. 22), the right to work (Art. 23), equal pay for equal work (*ibid.*), just and favorable remuneration (*ibid.*), the right to form and join trade unions (*ibid.*), the right to rest and leisure including limitations of working hours and periodic holidays with pay (Art. 24), an adequate standard of living (Art. 25), maternal and infant care (*ibid.*), the right to education (Art. 26). There are others that also reflect a concern with economic and social matters. Beyond those are guarantees more familiar to the Western world — the right to own property (Art. 17), freedom of thought, conscience, and religion (Art. 18), freedom of opinion and expression (Art. 19), freedom of peaceful assembly and association (Art. 20), the right to vote and equal suffrage (Art. 21), freedom of movement (Art. 13), protection against arbitrary interference with privacy (Art. 12), freedom from torture and cruel and inhuman punishment (Art. 5), freedom from slavery (Art. 4), equality before the law (Art. 7), presumption of innocence (Art. 11), and hearings before "an independent and impartial tribunal" (Art. 8).

The Declaration is hortatory, not an enforceable code. It is intended as a mere prelude to an international bill of rights. Though its main features and philosophy reflect attitudes and institutions of the West, not the East, it has been approved by all members of the United Nations except the Communist bloc, Saudi Arabia, and the Union of South Africa.

What effect it may have within the jurisdiction of each signatory nation is purely a domestic issue. What effect should be given it at the international level is a matter of earnest debate.

The General Assembly, which is restricted to passing resolutions and making recommendations, has played a limited role in protecting human rights. Some recommendations and resolutions have been in vain. For example, South Africa's response to a request from the General Assembly's Special Committee on Apartheid not to enforce certain death sentences was essentially that the matter was within its "domestic jurisdiction" in the meaning of Art. 2, par. 7 of the Charter. Despite numerous resolutions and constant heated debate in the General Assembly, the South African problem of apartheid remains unsolved, as does the similar situation in Rhodesia. Another example is the refusal of Hungary, Bulgaria, and Rumania to respect a General Assembly resolution concerning charges made by various Western governments that the countries had failed to abide by certain human rights provisions in the Paris Peace Treaties of 1947, to which the three countries were parties. The International Court of Justice, in an advisory opinion rendered upon the request of the General Assembly, held that the countries were required under the treaties to cooperate in examining the charges and to appoint representatives to Treaty Commissions established to investigate the matter. The countries, however, refused to comply.

In 1949 the General Assembly resolved that the Soviet Union had violated the UN Charter by refusing permission to Russian wives to leave the Soviet Union with their non-Russian husbands.

At the same time, however, the General Assembly has managed a formative approach to the interpretation and protection of human rights.

In 1961 the General Assembly, following its 1960 Declaration on the Granting of Independence to Colonial Countries and Peoples, established a Special Committee on Colonialism. That Committee has exercised wide prerogatives in examining and publicizing alleged instances of violations of human rights in dependent territories. The same procedures, involving publicity concerning written petitions submitted to the Committee and hearings of complainants, have been employed by the Special Committee on Apartheid. In addition, the General Assembly has not hesitated to invoke the principles of the Universal Declaration in dealing with numerous issues, such as freedom of information and the elimination of racial discrimination. And other organs concerned with human rights, such as the Economic and Social Council and the Commission on Human Rights, discharge their responsibilities under the supervision and authority of the General Assembly.

Other activities of the General Assembly in the human rights field include the drafting and approval of the various human rights covenants, which will be mentioned. In addition, the Assembly has promoted what might well be the most important aspect of the protection of human rights — educational programs and constructive discussions among governments. It has carried on, under the title of "advisory services in the field of human rights," a program of seminars and fellowships. The Senegal Conference, to which I shall refer, is one example. And from 1962 to 1965, a total of 158 fellowships in human rights were granted, mostly to Africans and Asians. Finally, the Assembly proclaimed 1968 as the International Year of Human Rights and encouraged member states and nongovernmental organizations to devote the year to "intensified efforts and understandings in the field of human rights, including an international review of achievements in this field" and to ratify the various Human Rights Conventions already approved. The General Assembly also decided to convene an international conference on human rights during 1968 to review the progress that has been made, evaluate the effectiveness of the methods used by the United Nations, and formulate and prepare a program of further measures to be taken.

A major role of the General Assembly, then, has been the education of nations and peoples regarding human rights. And education, it should be emphasized, is an extremely important aspect of promoting human rights in underdeveloped countries, whose vast indigenous populations often lack even general knowledge of fundamental guarantees.

The very existence of the Universal Declaration of Human Rights has had some internal effect in many countries. Space does not permit a catalog of all of the changes that have been made in the various countries to bring them into conformity with the precepts of the

Universal Declaration. They are extremely numerous and are summarized in the fifteen-odd volumes published by the United Nations each year in its *Yearbook on Human Rights*. Some of these are constitutional amendments and some are legislation. They cover a wide range: freedom of movement, the right to vote, freedom of peaceful assembly and association, laws relating to the activities of political parties, the right to petition for the redress of grievances, steps toward creating an independent judiciary, freedom of the press, treatment of prisoners, laws affecting marriage and family relationships, labor legislation, status of women, the right to education, and a wide variety of other matters.

There is, in addition, a proposal pending before the General Assembly to establish the office of High Commissioner of Human Rights whose main functions would be to keep in touch with world-wide developments in the area and to act as adviser and counsellor to nations that desire to bring their regimes into general conformity with the ideals of the Universal Declaration.

The desire of Americans in the early years for an independent judiciary sprang from a revulsion against the pressure exerted on the courts by the British colonial regime to serve British interests. Among these was the tremendous pressure exerted by customs officers to obtain the notorious writs of assistance which gave revenue agents broad and practically unfettered power to search houses and offices at will. The system was an evil one because the judges held their commissions at the will of the Crown and were dependent for their salaries on revenue collected from customs commissioners. Reported failures on their part to cooperate with the customs officials might deprive them of royal favor and result in their pay being reduced or stopped entirely. Or if they cooperated they might be rewarded. Some of the royal judges succumbed to these pressures; many did not. But the persistence and tenacity of customs in pursuing its campaign for these writs of assistance were responsible to a great degree for our determination to keep the courts free from executive control.

When independence came, the revulsion against the use of judges as political instruments turned into a mistrust of judges per se. The result was to salt the benches with laymen — what Lenin called "putting the jury on the bench." And that is what happened in the United States in the eighteenth century and in Russia in the twentieth. That practice in the States has largely ended, New Jersey finally eliminating all lay judges by her constitution of 1947. But in Vermont the custom still exists at the county court level. Each county court has one law-trained judge named by the legislature or governor and two laymen elected by the voters. These latter judges are called assistants or side judges. The status of the presiding judge is fixed by statute; the status of the lay judges is fixed by the state constitution. Hence they cannot be abolished except by constitutional amendment. The lay judges are not advisory; each has a vote. While they usually follow the law judge, they are free not to do so. And in recent times the two lay judges have overridden the law judge and have been sustained on appeal. They sit in both civil and criminal cases on the law side of the calendar; but they do not sit on the equity side.

Roots of the doctrine of judicial review by state courts of the constitutionality of Acts of state legislatures had their beginnings between the date of the American Revolution in 1776 and our constitutional convention in 1787, and by 1803 that power was fairly well established. The year 1803 is the Great Divide, for in that year Marshall, writing for a unanimous Court in *Marbury* v. *Madison,* 1 Cranch 137, asserted the authority of the Supreme Court to sit in judgment on the constitutionality of Acts of Congress. That decision, long debated by the scholars, is well entrenched. Beginning in 1821, the Court undertook to pass on the constitutionality of state courts' judgments (*Cohens* v. *Virginia,* 6 Wheat. 264). That authority has also been continuously exercised since that time. And it would seem that for the efficient operation of a federal system there must be a referee. Article VI of our Constitution makes the Constitution, the laws of the United States, and its treaties "the supreme law of the land"; and it adds "the Judges in every State shall be bound thereby, any thing in the Constitution or laws of any State to the contrary not withstanding." Thus the States cannot legislate in conflict with valid federal laws. And where the Constitution contains a "thou shalt not" directed to the States, some authority is needed to determine whether what a State says is permissible meets the federal standard. If this authority did not exist, we would often find that the parochial view of a State might override the national standard. Instead of having a grand design of a common market, we would be likely to find the States preferring local industry in a myriad of ways. Instead of having one, first-class citizenship, we might find some States relegating some minorities to a secondary status.

These considerations that lead to judicial review of state action do not apply of course to judicial review of Acts of Congress. Yet when the First Amendment says that Congress shall make no law "abridging the freedom of speech," how can judges sworn to support and defend the Constitution send a man to prison for violating an Act of Congress that forbids him from speaking? When the Fifth Amendment says no person shall be twice put in jeopardy of life or limb for the same offense, how can judges uphold a conviction obtained in violation of that guarantee against double jeopardy? And so the argument goes both at the federal and at the state levels.

Our federal judges are appointed for life ("good behavior") and the leverage over them through salary reduction is denied by the Constitution. Most of our state judges are elected, a pattern that Andrew Jackson promoted. That has its advantages and also its drawbacks. It means that a panel of state judges could not go against the tide of public prejudice on such issues as the racial one and survive the next election. Our state court judges have not, in other words, satisfied all the requirements of a truly independent judiciary. It is now a matter of history that the desegregation orders covering public schools, public parks, public utilities and allied facilities in places like Alabama, Louisiana, and Mississippi were orders of the federal district courts who were and are truly independent. In other words, but for federalism in the United States we would not be as far along toward solution of the racial minority problem as we are today. The federal structure provided the "equal protection" basis for the law. And the federal judiciary, named for life, were free to act without fear of reprisal.

Though much internal renovation has to take place in most nations, we could, I think, expect a great forward surge around the world, if the courts of each country were independent of executive or legislative control — and if the judges were also immune from domination by the prejudices of a majority of the community.

There are outstanding examples of this tradition in some of the newer, or so-called developing, nations.

The courts of Israel are a prime example. In one case, a person who qualified for deportation was taken under an order that was regular on its face. He was not, however, deported but held as if under arrest. That the Supreme Court would not tolerate, saying that "otherwise the liberties of the people of this country would be in real jeopardy."

The suspension of two Communist newspapers was set aside, not for lack of power, but for lack of appropriate exercise of that power. The ruling was that the mere tendency on the part of the papers to

endanger the public peace was not sufficient — there had to be prob-
ability that the public peace would be endangered.

The Israeli Supreme Court has handled issues involving conflicts
between the civil courts and military tribunals quite like some that
have arisen in this country. It held that once a person ceases to be a
soldier, he ceases on that date to be subject to a military tribunal even
for an offense committed while he was a soldier.

One Abu-Laben was detained by the Chief of Staff in the interests
of public security, public order, and national defense — a field in
which executive officers in England have been granted wide dis-
cretion. Under Israeli regulations the detention was, however, under
an advisory committee working with the Chief of Staff. At the time of
the detention no advisory committee had been appointed, though one
was brought into being before the hearing in the habeas corpus pro-
ceeding filed by Abu-Laben. The Court, ruling that the advisory committee was designed to protect the person detained, held that the detention was illegal and ordered the prisoner released.

A spirit of high regard for the dignity of the individual and deep
respect for principles of ordered liberty and justice permeate Israeli
judicial opinions. Its judiciary has indeed exalted the principles of a
Rule of Law as distinguished from a rule by the whim or caprice of
men.

The courtroom of the Israel Supreme Court in Jerusalem is plain,
not ornate — a quiet, dignified place. The court is not a tool of the
powers-that-be, or of the party in power, or of the head of the government. It is indeed an independent judiciary — the judges being
named for life, subject to removal for cause.

The Supreme Court of India has from the beginning sat in judgment on the constitutionality of actions of the states in the federation. Australia and Canada are in the same tradition; and so is the
Privy Council.

Out of Ceylon comes a recent decision holding that Parliament
may not create judicial tribunals at will but must follow the procedures of the Ceylon Constitution. The Ceylon Supreme Court also
held that an ex post facto law passed to punish participants in the
1962 abortive *coup d'etat* was an illegitimate legislative invasion of
judicial power under Ceylon's Constitution.

Out of India in 1964 came a historic decision. A nonmember of
the legislative assembly published a pamphlet critical of that body.

He was committed to prison for contempt by the assembly. He applied to the courts for relief by way of habeas corpus, and the judges of the high court released him on bail. The assembly forthwith took the publisher and his lawyer and the judges of the high court into custody for contempt of the assembly. The case reached the Supreme Court of India and a classic decision announced that the legislature was not competent to direct the production of the judges and the advocate before it or to call for an explanation for their actions, that it was competent for the judges to pass upon the legality of such restraints, and that their inquiry into it did not amount to contempt. This decision is historic not only on human rights but on separation of powers.

A catena of decisions by the Supreme Court of India makes clear that in that developing nation the tradition of an independent judiciary is already firmly entrenched.

Constitutional amendments in India are made by Parliament with the assent of the president, a vote of a majority of the total membership of each House, and a vote of not less than two-thirds of the members present and voting being necessary. But since such an amendment is a "law" and since no "law" which takes away or abridges the Fundamental Rights guaranteed by Article 13 of the Indian Constitution is valid, the Supreme Court of India held in 1967 that a parliamentary enactment, though in form a constitutional amendment, was unconstitutional if it altered one of the Fundamental Rights.

The principle of judicial independence is the philosophy behind the San Juan Declaration of Principles of the First Judicial Conference of the Americas in 1965. The San Juan Declaration proclaims in favor of "a stable judiciary, free from interference and pressure of any nature" and was signed by fourteen representatives of American judiciaries, thirteen being from Latin America. It resolved that a "vigorous and independent judiciary is a fundamental requisite, a basic element for the very existence of any society that respects the Rule of Law" and declared that "judicial independence should be secured by means of legal and constitutional guarantees that render impossible any interference or pressure of any nature with the judicial function." It also resolved that "judges should not be removed from office except for constitutionally established reasons and by due process of law."

Recognition of these principles at San Juan was a significant milestone, for in many Latin American nations judges are commonly ousted in *coup d'etats* and replaced by new ones who will do the dictator's bidding.

Of fifty-six underdeveloped nations, twenty-seven have constitutional provisions purporting to guarantee judicial independence. But of these, only eleven give judges the protection of tenure. These figures are suspect if taken as reflecting a practice of the executive and legislative branches in keeping hands off the judiciary. Though Ghana guaranteed tenure, Nkrumah had no difficulty in getting rid of the Justices of his Supreme Court. In December, 1963, Nkrumah, being unhappy at a decision of the Supreme Court, declared the decision "null and void." He thereupon revoked the appointment of Sir Arku Korsah as Chief Justice. At that time the Constitution provided that the President could remove the Chief Justice. But other Justices could be removed only by a Resolution of two-thirds of the Parliament for "misbehavior or infirmity of body or mind." By March, 1964, Nkrumah got a constitutional amendment passed that gave him power to dismiss judges "for reasons which appear to him sufficient." Following that amendment he removed four other Supreme Court justices.

On March 2, 1962, Ne Win, the dictator of Burma, put Myint Thein, who since 1957 had been Chief Justice of Burma, in prison and held him there until February 27, 1968, without any charge being preferred against him. Myint Thein, one of the most distinguished jurists of this century, believes in the Rule of Law and apparently was willing to entertain petitions for habeas corpus — an attitude intolerable to dictatorships.

Whenever a country has an independent judiciary, it has an inner strength which other countries do not know. Its independence means that justice is even-handed; that in the courts every minority knows equal justice under law; that no decision is the product of political expediency. The judiciary is, therefore, the great rock over which storms can break, leaving the country unshaken. Such a court gives security to a nation and its people and an unshaken faith in its principles.

Since that tradition has not been established in most nations, the question is whether some kind of federal protection of civil rights can be provided at the world level. The General Assembly has promoted this idea. Once the Declaration was proclaimed, the General Assembly instructed the various organizations of the United Nations to draft covenants of human rights which give international legal effect to the general principles in the Declaration.

Its agencies have been busy. Of the more than four hundred conventions prepared by those agencies, many touch human rights. The International Labor Organization that dates back to 1919 has been very active in proposing conventions in the area of human rights. One convention was designed to induce nations to eliminate company unions, antiunion discrimination in employment practices, and the like. Other conventions have covered hours of work, social security, reduction of the work week, the right to leisure, forced labor, and a vast array of related matters.

ILO has an ambitious procedure for policing its various fields of interest.

First, any association of employers or of workers may complain to ILO that a member state has not lived up to the requirements of a convention to which it is a party. In that event, ILO communicates the complaint to the nation in question, and invites it to make a statement on the subject. If no reply is received, or if an unsatisfactory one is returned, the Governing Body can publish the complaint and the reply, if any.

Second, any member state can file a complaint that it is not satisfied that another member state is observing a convention. In that event the governing body refers the complaint to a Commission of Enquiry. All member states are required to place at the disposal of the Commission of Enquiry all information relevant to the complaint. When the Commission of Enquiry has finished investigating, it prepares a report containing findings of fact and recommendations. This report is forwarded to the member states concerned, and they are supposed to inform ILO within three months whether they accept the recommendations, and if not, whether either proposes to refer the complaint to the International Court of Justice.

Third, the ILO Constitution provides that the decision of the International Court on any complaint referred to it is binding.

Fourth, if any member state fails to carry out any recommendations within the time prescribed, the governing Body may recommend such action as it may deem wise and expedient to secure compliance.

Although the formal dispute settlement procedure of the ILO Constitution, which contemplates one government filing a complaint against another government, has not been used frequently, there are instances where it has been employed successfully. A prime example is the Ghana-Portugal dispute of 1961. Ghana filed a complaint with the Director-General of the International Labor Office alleging that Portugal was not effectively securing observance of the Forced Labor Convention (which came into force in 1959) in certain overseas territories. The Governing Body of the Office referred the complaint to a Commission of Enquiry pursuant to Article 26 of the ILO Constitution.

After considering written submissions by the parties involved and also by other governments and nongovernmental organizations, the Commission heard testimony from witnesses produced by both Ghana and Portugal. The Commission also visited two of the overseas Portuguese territories involved, and questioned workers, management staff, and public officials. In 1962, the Commission issued a report, in which it set forth findings of fact and recommended certain remedial measures. Shortly thereafter, the parties indicated to the Governing Body that they accepted the Commission's findings and recommendations.

The actions taken by Portugal in accordance with its agreement to implement the Commission's recommendations have been evaluated continuously by scrutiny of Portuguese reports concerning the territories involved, and by discussion of the subject in the ILO's Conference Committee on the Application of Conventions and Recommendations. In November, 1965, the Governing Body requested Portugal to submit during 1966 a full report on the measures taken to implement the Commission's recommendations. Portugal complied with this request and submitted a report in January, 1966. A special Committee, appointed by the Governing Body to examine the report, found that some recommendations had been implemented satisfactorily, and that progress, ranging from considerable to slow, had occurred in implementing the remaining recommendations.

These procedures therefore fall short of coercion in the customary sense of law. But in practice they have been widely effective in developing a consensus in many troubled areas.

The work of ILO means that more and more international labor standards have been adopted, that a whole network of international commitments have been entered into by governments on behalf of and in favor of their workers.

In late 1967, the General Assembly issued a Declaration on Women's Rights calling for the end of discrimination between men and women in all phases of life. The prior convention on the Political

Rights of Women guarantees women the equal right with men to vote, to be eligible for election, to be entitled to hold public office, and to exercise all public functions. The later Declaration, although guaranteeing these same political rights, directs a general elimination of any discrimination between men and women in all walks of life — political, social, economic, cultural, legal, educational, and marital. Article 2 of the Declaration states that "All appropriate measures shall be taken to abolish existing laws, customs, regulations and practices which are discriminatory against women, and to establish adequate legal protection for equal rights of men and women, . . ." And Article 3 provides that "All appropriate measures shall be taken to educate public opinion and direct national aspirations toward the eradication of prejudice and the abolition of customary and all other practices which are based on the idea of the inferiority of women." Like the Universal Declaration of Human Rights, however, the Declaration on Women's Rights was not designed to be a binding agreement, but rather a statement of intent.

The various Human Rights Conventions sponsored by the General Assembly have covered a wide range of subjects.

The Convention on the Prevention and Punishment of the Crime of Genocide came into force in 1951, some seventy states having become parties.

The Convention Relating to the Status of Refugees came into force in 1954, some fifty-four states having become parties.

The Convention Relating to the Status of Stateless Persons came in force in 1960, eighteen states having become parties.

The Convention on the Political Rights of Women came into force in 1954, over fifty states having become parties.

The Convention on the Nationality of Married Women came into force in 1958, nearly forty states having become parties.

The Convention on Consent to Marriage, Minimum Age for Marriage, and Registration of Marriages came into force in 1964, some seventeen states having become parties.

The Convention on the International Right of Correction (of news dispatches considered false or distorted) came into force in 1964, seven states having become parties.

The Slavery Convention of September 25, 1926, as amended by a 1953 protocol, came into force in 1953, over sixty states becoming parties

A Supplementary Convention on Slavery came into force in 1957, some sixty states having become parties.

The Convention concerning Discrimination in Employment and Occupation (ILO sponsored) came into force in 1960, some fifty states becoming parties.

The Convention Concerning Equal Remuneration for Men and Women Workers for Work of Equal Value (an ILO convention) came into effect in 1953, some fifty states becoming parties.

The Convention Concerning Freedom of Association and Protection of the Right to Organize (ILO sponsored) came into force in 1950, over seventy states becoming parties.

The Convention Against Discrimination in Education (sponsored by UNESCO) came into force in 1962, over thirty states becoming parties.

Additional protocols for some of these conventions are still awaiting ratification by member states.

There are in addition several conventions awaiting approval:

(1) The Convention on the Reduction of Statelessness — 1961,
(2) The Convention on the Elimination of All Forms of Racial Discrimination — 1965,
(3) The International Covenant on Economic, Social and Cultural Rights — 1966,
(4) The International Covenant on Civil and Political Rights — 1966.

Of these, the last is the most pervasive and the most important. It covers a wide range of civil and political rights — self-determination, equal protection, prohibition of uncivil, inhuman, or degrading punishment, restriction of capital punishment, abolition of slavery, a ban on arbitrary arrest or detention, prompt arraignment, judicial inquiry into legality of arrests, freedom of travel, abolition of imprisonment for debt, public trials by "a competent, independent and impartial tribunal," presumption of innocence, right to counsel, speedy trial, prohibition of ex post facto laws, religious liberty, freedom of thought and expression, peaceful assembly, freedom of association and so on. It will become effective after thirty-five nations have ratified it or acceded to it.

The enforcement machinery centers in a Human Rights Committee of eighteen members chosen by the signatory states. They will be paid for their services by the General Assembly and their staff will be provided by the Secretary General.

The signatory states make reports to the Committee on the measures they adopt to give effect to the rights covered by the covenant and the progress made in enforcing those guarantees.

One signatory state may file a complaint against another signatory state that the latter is not fulfilling its obligations under the Covenant. If the matter is not adjusted to the satisfaction of both states, either may refer the matter to the Committee. The Committee shall make available its "good offices" to the parties with a view to a "friendly solution." Failing that, the Committee is directed to make a report on the facts alone. If the dispute is not resolved in that fashion, the Committee may, with the prior consent of the states involved, appoint a five-man Conciliation Commission, on which the states in dispute are not represented.

The Commission will seek an amicable settlement. Failing that, it makes a report on the facts of the case and its views "on the possibilities of an amicable solution." From this time on, any resolution of the conflict turns on a consensual agreement of the states who are parties to the dispute. There is, in other words, no enforcement machinery.

An optional protocol to this Covenant provides that an individual who claims to be a victim of a violation by a signatory state may file his complaint with the Committee. The Protocol provides:

> The Committee shall not consider any communication from an individual unless it has ascertained that:
> (a) The same matter is not being examined under another procedure of international investigation or settlement;
> (b) The individual has exhausted all available domestic remedies. This shall not be the rule where the application of the remedies is unreasonably prolonged.

The Committee brings the complaint to the attention of the state charged with wrongplay. After receiving its reply and ascertaining the facts, the Committee "shall forward its views to the State Party concerned and to the individual." Here again there is no enforcement machinery. Both the Covenant and the Protocol are dependent on publicity, soft pressure, and conciliation as the means of enforcement. And, based on experiences under other conventions, these devices are often adequate.

Some of the recent conventions proposed by the General Assembly provide that in case of unsettled disputes, the meaning and construction of the conventions shall be referred "at the request of one of the parties to the dispute" to the International Court of Justice. This is true, for example, of the latest convention on the abolition of slavery which the Soviet Union and eight of the Eastern European nations have joined, and of the Convention on Political Rights of Women which they have also joined. The Slavery Convention in Article 9 provides "no reservations may be made," a prohibition which the Soviets have officially recognized. But the Soviets, as well as the other Eastern European nations, have lodged a reservation against the compulsory jurisdiction provision in the Convention on the Political Rights of Women. Thus, in spite of the Soviets' refusal to accept the general jurisdiction of the International Court of Justice, they have made an exception respecting the latest Slavery Convention.

Regional systems for the enforcement of human rights also show great promise. One of the most significant developments took place in the early 1950's under the statute of the Council of Europe. That statute established a European Council consisting of a Committee of Ministers, a Consultative Assembly, and a Secretariat, to promote economic and social progress in Europe and to safeguard and realize the ideals and principles forming a common heritage among European nations. Article 1 (b) of the Statute provided that this aim was to be "pursued through the organs of the Council by discussion of questions of common concern and by agreements and common action in economic, social, cultural, scientific, legal, and administrative matters and in the maintenance and further realisation of human rights and fundamental freedoms." At the first session of the Consultative Assembly, that body recommended that the Committee of Ministers assume responsibility for the drafting of a human rights convention. When finally a convention was drafted, it established both a European Commission of Human Rights and a European Court of Human Rights to enforce various legal rights other than the right to habeas corpus. This Convention included ten rights from the Universal Declaration of the United Nations: security of the person, freedom from slavery and servitude, freedom from arbitrary arrest, detention, or exile, and the right to a fair trial, freedom from arbitrary interference in one's family life, freedom of thought, conscience, and religion, freedom of opinion and expression, freedom of assembly, freedom of association, freedom to unite in trade unions, and finally, the right to marry and found a family.

This Convention has been ratified by fifteen European nations and their agencies, and has been in force since 1954. The Commission of Human Rights acts as an administrative agency that seeks to obtain a friendly settlement in the case, if possible. It makes a report on the case and states its opinion as to whether the Convention has been breached. This report goes to the Ministers of the Council which must decide by a two-thirds majority whether there has been a violation of the Convention. The referral of a case to the Court may be either by the Commission itself, by the signatory nation whose national is alleged to be a victim, by the signatory nation which referred the case to the Commission, or by the signatory against which the complaint is drawn. Moreover, the jurisdiction of the Court depends on whether or not the signatories involved either have agreed to accept the jurisdiction of the court as compulsory or have agreed to a particular *ad hoc* submission of a case. Of the fifteen signatories, eleven have subscribed to the compulsory jurisdiction of the court. These eleven include the United Kingdom, which submitted to compulsory jurisdiction for three years beginning January 14, 1966. And in 1967, the United Kingdom extended to twenty-one overseas territories the right of individual application.

By the end of September, 1967, the Commission had received seven complaints brought by one member state against another, and 3,350 complaints brought against states by individuals. Actually, the seven interstate cases relate only to three grievances — two complaints against the United Kingdom by Greece concerning Cyprus; a complaint against Italy by Austria; and four almost identical complaints against Greece by Denmark, Sweden, Norway, and the Netherlands.

The Austrain complaint against Italy concerned criminal proceedings, which Austria claimed were incompatible with the Convention, resulting in the conviction of six men for the murder of an Italian customs officer that took place in the German-speaking part of South Tyrol. This application was declared admissible; and in 1963 the Commission reported to the Committee of Ministers that in its view there had been no violation of the Convention. The Committee of Ministers affirmed this finding.

When the military junta took over Greece, the Danish, Norwegian, Dutch and Swedish governments lodged an application against Greece with the Commission. An investigation was launched and it was hoped that it would be completed early in 1968, the Council being particularly concerned about the fate of those Greeks who are members of the Consultative Assembly. The Council promptly resolved that it:

> Holds itself ready to make a declaration at the appropriate time on the possibility of the suspension of Greece from, or her right to remain a member of the Council of Europe;
> Urgently requests the Bureau to spare no effort to obtain information, in particular on the fate of the appointed Greek members of the Assembly, and to secure for them treatment compatible with humanity, justice and law.

The complaining governments allege that the present Greek government has violated its obligations under the Convention by suspending certain Articles of the Greek Constitution, an action which is not justified by Article 15 of the Convention (allowing a government to derogate from certain obligations in times of emergency).

The Consultative Assembly of the Council met in Strasbourg in 1968 and reviewed a report prepared by two Assembly members — Siegmann (Dutch) and Silkin (U.K.) — who had recently visited Greece and conducted interviews with various Greek leaders. Siegmann and Silkin concluded that Greece was under dictatorial rule, but reported that they had received "assurances by present Greek leaders" that by September, 1968, a new constitution would be submitted to a referendum and that elections would follow. After lengthy debate, based largely on this report, the Consultative Assembly adopted a Resolution stating that "if Greece intends to remain a Member of the Council of Europe she will have to return without delay to a regime which is democratic and parliamentary and respectful of human rights and fundamental freedoms as required by the Statute of the Council," and that a new constitution "should be truly democratic and promulgated, applied and followed by free elections at the earliest possible date." The Resolution goes on to provide that the Assembly intends to "assist Greece to return to the road to democracy," that to this end the Assembly will closely examine and make observations on the proposed Greek Constitution once it is drawn up and made available, that it will make every effort to ensure that the referendum on the constitution takes place by September, 1968, at the latest, under free conditions, and that it considers the spring of 1969 as the latest date at which a democratic and parliamentary system of government should operate again in Greece.

The Assembly, moreover, was of the view that "following the applications lodged by the Danish, Norwegian, Swedish, and Netherlands Governments respectively, it is for the European Commission of Human Rights to express an opinion on whether the provisions of the Convention on Human Rights have been violated."

With respect to the individual complaints, submitted to the Commission, about 95 per cent of them have been declared inadmissible or deleted from the list of cases without being communicated to the government concerned. Thus, only about 140 individual cases have proceeded beyond preliminary examination. Of these, about 90 were rejected after the observations of the government concerned had been obtained. The remaining 50 complaints were declared admissible, and have either been disposed of or are still pending. And, as in the case of the interstate complaints, some of the individual cases fall into groups.

None of the interstate cases has reached the court; and only five of the individual cases have come to that judicial body. One of the five was struck off the list by the court when new legislation by the government concerned brought its laws into line with the Convention. In a second case, the court affirmed the Commission's finding that there had been no violation of the Convention. Another case, raising the issue whether the linguistic system for education in Belgium was incompatible with the Convention (the Commission answered in the affirmative), is pending before the court and has been scheduled for a hearing on the merits. The remaining two cases pending before the court, which were set for a hearing for January, 1968, raise the question whether the period of detention spent by two prisoners in Germany and Austria violate those provisions of the Convention guaranteeing the right to a trial within a reasonable time and to a hearing within a reasonable time to determine whether there is any criminal charge.

The essence of the work is reflected by the Commission, not by the court. It is the agency that seeks to settle the cases and bring about by friendly acquiescence a change in the practice that gave rise to the complaints. It has had, I think, a healthy influence in providing a place where complaints can be aired and in providing an agency of inquiry or oversight that makes most bureaucracies more cautious.

The Universal Declaration of Human Rights was drafted before the recent proliferation of new nations, particularly in Africa. The document reflects largely the viewpoint of the Western developed countries. As a result, the new countries of Africa — with traditions and philosophies of life different from the Western states — face problems in attempting to implement some of the guarantees outlined in the Declaration. The underdeveloped countries of the entire Third World, for that matter, have difficulty trying to adapt those guarantees to a society of backward and illiterate people and an economic system in which poverty and starvation are the rule rather than the exception.

At a conference held at Dakar, Senegal, in early 1966, representatives of most of the African countries discussed the problems they share in enforcing the provisions of the Universal Declaration and the subsequent human rights conventions. Many African states, upon achieving their independence, expressed in constitutional form their adherence to the principles of the Declaration. This is particularly true of the former French colonies. At least seventeen African states have incorporated the Universal Declaration into their constitutions in some form, for example, by reciting adherence to it in the preamble. The constitutions of some other African states contain guarantees which are clearly drawn from the Declaration. Moreover, in May, 1963, this acceptance of the Universal Declaration was reaffirmed in the Charter of the Organization of African Unity, established by some thirty African governments.

Despite this seemingly overwhelming acceptance of the principles of the Universal Declaration, representatives at the Senegal Conference expressed varying opinions of the content and scope of that document, and some reservations concerning how effective international implementation of the rights it seeks to confer might be realized. The problems faced by African countries in enforcing the Declaration's guarantees stem primarily from the fact that the Declaration represents the political philosophy of the Western developed nations. To be sure, the effects of colonialism still linger, and domination of the African countries by the Western powers has instilled some Western values into African life. Yet, the economic needs of these underdeveloped nations assume paramount importance, and tribal and religious traditions are ever present in the background.

The Senegal Conference proceedings revealed that the African countries were practically unanimous in condemning governmental actions that interfered with certain basic freedoms — such as practices of slavery, torture, or cruel and degrading punishment, and deprivation of the right to a fair trial. Because of the enormous problems of economic development, however, participants at the Conference emphasized the necessity of accommodating the concepts of the Universal Declaration with the urgent needs of the African states. The Declaration, for example, guarantees the right of everyone to choose his employment freely and enjoy just conditions of work. But Africa faces a dilemma due to its heavy problems of unemployment and underdevelopment. Some measure of state intervention has been necessary to control employment and channel talents into appropriate occupational areas.

A similar problem exists by reason of the guarantee of the right to own property. African countries have found it necessary to place some restrictions on the right, particularly with respect to foreign investment and programs of land reform. Such measures are consistent, however, with the African tradition of property — historically property was viewed as communal in nature. The concept of property ownership expressed in the Declaration may not be a realistic standard to apply to the needs of these countries, or of any nation of the Third World. Although the Senegal conferees recognized the right to own property as inviolable in principle, the right should be considered a social function to be exercised for the good of the community, or at least in such a manner as not to conflict with the requirements of economic development.

Other problems were noted which prevented strict implementation of the Universal Declaration. Some interference by the state in the dissemination of news and information was often made necessary by the fact that generally only the state possessed the necessary capital and resources to invest in establishing communication and information services. Implementation of the right to education runs into large obstacles in Africa — the effects of discrimination in education during the colonial period, the lack of financial resources to support effective educational systems coupled with the population explosion, the shortage of qualified teachers, the heavy influx of refugees in certain countries, and in some instances even the language of instruction.

Participants at the Senegal Conference were generally agreed that the Universal Declaration did not in every case provide viable rules for African society. Consequently, they emphasized that African participation in international machinery for enforcing human rights would have to be preceded by recognition in non-African countries of the nature of social, political, and economic life in Africa, and would depend upon the willingness of non-African states to adjust the interpretation and application of the Declaration to African society.

The possibility of establishing a regional African enforcement mechanism similar to that of Europe is also discussed in African circles. But a counterweight to that proposal is the jealousy with which the new African countries, just freed from the strictures of colonialism, guard their independence. Limitations on sovereignty are viewed with distrust. Because of this reluctance to abandon the sovereignty newly won, bilateral or multilateral agreements are often suggested as a first step toward an eventual, broadbased African regional mechanism. Enforcement machinery developed by and responsible to Africa itself would, of course, adapt the basic principles of the Universal Declaration to the unique nature of African society.

The problems faced by the Asian and Southeast Asian countries in developing a regional mechanism for enforcement of human rights seem much more complex than those in Africa. The heterogeneous nature of Asian society is one reason. Politically, governments range from communism to Western-oriented democracies. Ethnically, there are some countries, such as Japan, where almost all the people speak the same language and possess the same cultural traditions, but there are others sharply divided by language and cultural barriers. Religious, racial, and cultural discrimination present serious problems in those latter countries. In some states, such as in Ceylon and Japan, the spectre of poverty and starvation is not an acute problem. In others, such as China and India, merely having enough food to exist is considered a blessing.

Moreover, as already noted, the history of Asian countries differs markedly from that of Western nations. Asian societies are ruled largely by tradition — their past, except for recent colonial periods, has been one of absolute rulers, rigid social institutions governed by custom, and the pervading influence of various religions. As in Africa, the loosening or termination of foreign control and domination in many of the Asian countries has produced a strong sense of nationalism and a jealous pride in newly gained sovereignty, even though religion, language, and culture often cross national lines.

Complicating the picture even more is the distrust of a Rule of Law in some countries — for example, Korea. And those societies influenced by Chinese philosophy consider a virtuous ruler to be the best guarantee of order, rather than an enduring set of laws.

Many Asian states, drawing from Western experience, adopted written constitutions, some of which contain certain guarantees of fundamental rights. Yet, in many cases, the guarantees exist as a practical matter only on paper; and effective implementation is nonexistent. In some countries, free elections, freedom of expression and association, and other rights are severely limited. And, as in Africa, the pressing burdens of underdevelopment and tremendous human suffering have required restrictions on Western-formulated economic and property rights.

These factors, however, have not prevented proposals designed to encourage Asian states to adopt regional mechanisms to enforce human rights. For example, an Advisory Group of the South-East Asian and Pacific Conference of Jurists recommended in 1965 that steps be taken toward regional recognition and enforcement of human rights. The Advisory Group expressed the opinion that only political and civil rights should be dealt with in an initial convention because of the tremendous differences in current social and economic conditions, both in Asia and among the states in the Pacific area. The mechanism of enforcement would, of course, have to take into account the traditional method of settling disputes in Asian countries. A judicial system comparable to that of Europe would not be acceptable, at least in the beginning, since Asian societies have historically settled disputes through techniques of conciliation, such as the good offices of a third party. The Advisory Group also suggested the possibility of beginning regional cooperation on a small scale — among countries that might find it relatively easier to cooperate with one or two neighbors than on a wider basis. But however modest a beginning might be, there is hope that despite serious obstacles even the nations of Asia might find it possible to cooperate in this all-important field of human rights.

Latin America presents still different problems in establishing and maintaining an effective system for implementation of human rights guarantees. The nations of South and Central America — often termed the "oldest of the new nations" — have existed in the ever present shadow of the United States. The political policy of nonintervention — whose roots can be traced to President Monroe — is still a powerful force. The philosophy of Latin American theorists such as Alvarez, Drago, and Calvo constituted the moving force behind the absolute doctrine of nonintervention (which, after the 1930's, even the United States purported to recognize without claiming an

exception for itself) which is embodied in Article 15 of the Charter of
the Organization of American States. It is still a resounding force in
spite of what we did in Cuba and in the Dominican Republic in 1961
and 1965 respectively.

But our philosophy of nonintervention is not the only obstacle to
effective development of regional mechanisms to protect human
rights in Latin America. For the most part, our Southern neighbors
possess primitive judicial machinery. Dictators, violence, and armed
hostilities are frequent. And the use or threat of force for the assump-
tion of political power presents a too-ready alternative to the ballot
box. Although much has been said of Latin American "solidarity,"
the nations of the region are by no means unified — either among
themselves or within their own borders.

It is not surprising, then, that at least until very recently the American states have not actively promoted the enforcement of human
rights at a regional level. The OAS Charter mentions individual
rights only in passing, as if it were just a formality to be observed.
And although the Charter was followed closely in time by the American Declaration of Rights and Duties of Man, the latter document has
until recently remained only a pious statement.

Perhaps the most significant push given human rights in Latin
America was the Declaration of Santiago that emerged from the Fifth
Meeting of Consultation of Ministers of Foreign Affairs at Santiago,
Chile, in 1959. In that document, the American states took the first
steps toward achieving some type of regional consensus with respect
to human rights and methods of enforcement. From the meeting at
Santiago emerged the Inter-American Commission on Human Rights,
established to promote the observance of human rights in the Americas. The Commission was handicapped, however, by the absence
of a definitive statement of its powers. Article 1 of the statute establishing the Commission states that the Commission is to be "an autonomous entity of the Organization of American States, the function of
which is to promote respect for human rights." In its original form,
Article 9 stated that the Commission's duties were:

—to develop an awareness of human rights among the peoples of
   America;
—to make recommendations to the governments of the member states
   in general, if it considers such action advisable, for the adoption of
   progressive measures in favor of human rights within the framework of their domestic legislation and, in accordance with their

constitutional precepts, appropriate measures to further the faithful observance of those rights;

—to prepare such studies or reports as it considers advisable in the performance of its duties;

—to urge the governments of the member states to supply it with information on the measures adopted by them in matters of human rights;

—to serve the Organization of American States as an advisory body in respect of human rights.

Despite this rather vague language and the lack of a grant of effective powers to implement observance of human rights, the Commission played a surprisingly important role in the recent disturbances in the Dominican Republic. It was also quite active during the months following the 1961 abortive Bay of Pigs invasion. Its ability to survive and contribute despite its vague status can be attributed largely to the ingenuity of its members. Although until 1965 the Commission possessed no express power to entertain and examine individual petitions submitted to it, the Commission decided that under its statute it could receive and take note of communications from individuals and use them as a basis for making observations on human rights to an individual country. Formal authority to entertain such petitions was finally granted by the Second Special Inter-American Conference held at Rio de Janeiro in late 1965. The Conference resolved that the Commission should be authorized to "examine communications submitted to it and any other available information, so that it may address to the government of any American state a request for information deemed pertinent by the Commission, and so that it may make recommendations, when it deems this appropriate, with the objective of bringing about more effective observance of fundamental human rights." The substance of this resolution was embodied in an addition to Article 9 of the Commission's statute.

The 1959 Santiago meeting also increased hopes that one or more covenants would eventually govern human rights in the Americas in a manner similar to that adopted in the European community. The Declaration of Santiago requested the Inter-American Council of Jurists to prepare a draft convention on human rights and a draft agreement establishing an Inter-American Court for the Protection of Human Rights. The Council of Jurists quickly drafted the documents, which emerged quite similar in scope and machinery to the European Convention, but no important action was taken on the draft convention until the 1965 Rio Conference. At that conference, the draft convention was sent to the Council of the Organization of American States for consideration and possible revision, and then submitted to the governments concerned for suggestions. As of November, 1967, the Commission on Human Rights — whose views had been solicited by the Council — had recommended some major changes in the draft. For example, the European system whereby member states can submit complaints but individuals can do so only pursuant to an optional protocol was turned upside down. Under the Commission's recommendation, individuals are given the right to petition, but states are permitted to do so only pursuant to an optional protocol.

A Latin American version of a regional human rights program may well differ greatly from the European model in its final form. As I have said, Latin American countries, like the United States, are highly sensitive to questions of national sovereignty. The pressing requirements of economic development and the political turmoil that either exists in or threatens most of the countries to the south get priority. And since it is probably a practical impossibility to secure widespread adoption of an effective system for the protection of human rights without the full and ready participation of the United States, this country's reluctance to entrust protection of the human rights of its citizens to other than its own tribunals represents perhaps the most formidable barrier to a regional system.

Yet, despite these difficulties, progress in the direction of regional cooperation and enforcement has been made. The nations of the hemisphere may yet recognize in practice, as well as in principle, the view expressed in the Declaration of Santiago that peace in the American states "can be effective only insofar as human rights and fundamental freedoms and the exercise of representative democracy are a reality within each one of them."

In general, apart from the European Convention, it appears that the great bugaboo of sovereignty still blocks any bold steps toward international implementation of human rights. Moreover, the feeling of the Third World nations that the Universal Declaration perhaps is at least in some respects not relevant to their societies lessens the chance that effective enforcement of human rights could at present be approached more broadly than on a regional level. But even that is a great beginning. Regional enforcement machinery possesses advantages, since the states of the region selected would possess common characteristics and could adapt the principles of the Universal Declaration to their societies.

Arguments over sovereignty often defeat at the very threshold any proposal for an international remedy. This bugaboo, however, has been overcome hundreds of times in international arrangements. It is always overcome whenever there is a consensus between two or more nations who decide to work together rather than go it alone. One of the most conspicuous and successful examples is the Universal Postal Union established in 1870, already mentioned. It has had a rather distinguished career in bringing a regime of peaceful existence to various diverse and competing nations. Its existence is today an indispensable element for the world community and its business transactions — indeed to the whole international political life of contemporary society.

All states need not be merged into one great world state in order that the legality of their conduct may be inquired into and examined. The European Commission of Human Rights and the European Court of Human Rights is one illustration. The treaties, worked out by the United Nations, are another approach. Regional agreements are still another. Either can define the standards of International Due Process and provide enforcement machinery.

One of the most effective ways of providing enforcement machinery for a regime of International Due Process would be the international or regional writ of habeas corpus to enforce all or selected guarantees contained in the Universal Declaration of Human Rights. A part of the machinery created by treaties could be either an International Court of Habeas Corpus or Regional Habeas Corpus courts where lawyers would either prosecute or oppose applications for the writ. What category of human rights could be brought within the purview of an International or Regional Court of Habeas Corpus would be a matter for political decision. Views will differ as to what rights should be declared fundamental. A full-blown galaxy cannot be expected overnight but there can be beginnings, and perhaps the best starting point is one suggested by Luis Kutner, namely, "arbitrary arrests."

If individuals may be arrested or incarcerated without cause or for causes which conceivably violate fundamental human rights, they do not have the most elementary fundamental freedom.

Another possibility would be to hitch habeas corpus to Article X of the Declaration of Human Rights. Article X provides:

Everyone is entitled in full equality to a fair and public hearing by by an independent and impartial tribunal, in the determination of his rights and obligations and of any criminal charge against him.

Or the rule of our *Milligan* case (4 Wall. 2) that a military commission may not be substituted for a civil trial in a geographical area where the civil government and the civil courts can operate might be adopted and habeas corpus made available as a writ to remedy the evil of mounting military regimes across the world.

Still another possibility would be to use habeas corpus to challenge the legality of detention of an individual in a condition of slavery, outlawed by Article 4 of the Declaration:

No one shall be held in slavery or servitude; slavery and the slave trade shall be prohibited in all their forms.

We know from various reports (the investigators for the Council of Europe and from Amnesty International, a private group that has a consultative status with the Council) that many Greeks have been jailed, placed in camps, put under surveillance, or subjected to house arrest. The exact number is not known though by the end of January, 1968, they totalled at least 3,000. Of these, hardly 15 per cent were Communists. Many are old and infirm who were arrested on security files prepared twenty years ago. They came from all walks of life.

Torture of prisoners by military police is common. Cruel beatings, sexual torture, electric shock, and nonphysical torture, such as placement in vermin-ridden cells, threats to kill, maim, and rape, mock executions, and the signing of declarations denouncing family and beliefs are common methods of "aiding interrogation."

There is extensive "bugging" and censorship. Freedom of the press has disappeared. To whom can these prisoners turn? At present there is no tribunal that is not under the control of the very forces persecuting them. Some world protection must be found for prisoners such as these — suspected and arbitrarily arrested for their beliefs, held without trial, and tortured until they break or die.

The generality of many of the UN pronouncements on human rights brings unanimity in their approval. Once the general proposition is reduced to specifics, agreement is less than unanimous. When the remedy is through publicity and informal discussion, which is the pattern of UN activity, there is wide international cooperation. When enforcement is proposed, the resistance mounts. But the need is great for a UN court or commission or regional courts or commissions passing on concrete cases and building a mosaic of case law that all can see and understand.

It will be said that no international remedy could be effective because the borders of each nation would be barred to any international agency bent on enforcement. The initial question, however, is whether a consensus can be reached whereby an international agency can be created (a) to investigate the charge, and (b) to make a report containing its findings and its recommendations.

Individuals would have a remedy in this international tribunal only on a showing either that their own nation provided no remedy or that the remedy, though available at home, had been wrongfully withheld from them.

This new regime would create a state-federal relation, albeit a tenuous one. It would rest on a civilized conception of International Due Process of law that had been hammered out at conference tables between the various nations.

Though there would be no sheriff's posse to execute the order of the international agency, there would be the force of publicity and the power of world opinion behind any report and proposed remedy. World opinion may not be easily rallied around the abstract concept of arbitrary arrests. But it can be rallied, and will be if there is an appropriate procedure, against the long detention of an outstanding author or poet or a distinguished jurist, or another human where the crime is not violence but intellectual, religious, or political expression.

Domestic orders of courts are sometimes challenged and defied, and even in our own country there are historic examples where some have gone unenforced. Yet by and large the concensus to live under the law in time makes most decisions self-enforcing. In this sensitive area of human rights at the international level there can, I think, be no doubt but that a judgment of an international agency that a person is being unlawfully detained or has been unconstitutionally tried in light of the standards of international due process would be a powerful force in the lives of all of us.

The work of the International Commission of Jurists — the private organization that goes around the world probing into troubled hu-

man rights spots — is revealing. The publicity that its reports bring
have had a profound effect. No nation, no tribunal likes to be depicted
to the world in uncivilized terms.

Australia, early in the history of the United Nations, proposed an
International Court of Human Rights to hear all disputes concerning
the rights and freedoms provided for in the Declaration of Human
Rights. Under that proposal individuals could file complaints with
the Court, as could a State. Moreover, the Court would have appellate
jurisdiction over "all decisions of the courts of the States bound by the
obligations contained in the Declaration of Human Rights, in which
any question arises as to the rights of citizenship or the enjoyment of
human rights, or fundamental freedoms." The Australian proposal
provided that any judgment or order by the International Court of
Human Rights "shall be enforced in and by the State affected by the
judgment or order." The judges, who were to be not less than three
in number, were to be elected in the fashion of the judges of the International Court of Justice.

A corollary was a proposal for the creation of a Standing Committee (or Commission) to receive complaints from individuals concerning human rights and to seek settlement of them. Only after it had
failed would a case go to some international court for trial — either
to a new International Court of Human Rights or to a panel of the
International Court of Justice.

These efforts never came to fruition in large part due to the opposition of the Great Powers. Thus in 1953 Secretary of State Dulles set
this nation on the path of voluntary procedures of "persuasion, education, and example rather than formal undertakings which commit
one part of the world to impose its particular social and moral standards upon another part of the world community, which has different
standards."

Although divergent in a great many other areas, the Soviet and
American positions with regard to the establishment of international
mechanisms to enforce human rights are quite alike. Both countries
do not hesitate to invoke the limitation in the Charter that the United
Nations shall not interfere in matters essentially within the domestic
jurisdiction of a state. And Russia's failure to declare its acceptance
of the compulsory general jurisdiction of the International Court of
Justice is closely paralleled by the approach of our Connally Amendment.

Resistance on the part of Russia to organized international con-

trol over implementation of human rights agreements, except by submission in specific instances, is predicated in part on the stated belief
that once a State enters into an international agreement, it should be
assumed that it will honor that agreement. She considers constant
policing by foreign states as undesirable. Thus, the official Soviet text-
book on international law states that agreements should not "contain
clauses establishing any supra-State agencies dealing with human
rights and having legislative, administrative or judicial functions."
And the Soviet delegate to the Third Committee, in which the text of
draft human rights conventions has been discussed, announced that
in the Russian view:

> [m]easures of implementation should be founded on the obligation
> of States to adopt appropriate internal legislative, administrative,
> social and other measures for the maintenance and protection of
> human rights. That obligation together with the additional obligation
> of States to inform the United Nations regularly of the measures they
> are taking in conformity with the Covenants would form a proper
> basis for achieving the human rights provided for in the Covenants.

The Russians and John Foster Dulles saw eye to eye on this issue.

American reluctance to accept international control over human
rights violations, and for that matter even to ratify most human rights
conventions, has centered around the assertion that regulation of
disputes over fundamental guarantees between a government and its
own citizens is a matter of domestic concern; in other words, the
rights of American nationals can be and should be protected by American tribunals. Beginning in the 1950's, the United States delegation to
the UN announced that we had decided not to sign or ratify the various
covenants on human rights that were being discussed. Hence our
delegates took little part in the discussions.

John Foster Dulles, the foremost preacher of this gospel, said in
1953 that the administration was of the view that treaties should not
be "used as a device to circumvent the constitutional procedures established in relation to what are essentially matters of domestic concern." He followed this statement by noting, with respect to proposed
human rights treaties, that although the administration intended to
"encourage the promotion everywhere of human rights and individual freedoms," it preferred, as noted, voluntary procedures. This
position was repudiated by the Kennedy administration in 1963; but
the Dulles philosophy produced an infection in our foreign policy

that has remained virulent, and has played no small part in preventing United States ratification of most UN human rights conventions.

There are some minor breaks in the wall. The Senate, on November 2, 1967, gave its advice and consent to the Supplemental Slavery Convention, without reservation even though compulsory jurisdiction of the International Court of Justice is provided. President Johnson signed our accession on November 9, and an instrument of ratification was deposited with the UN on December 6. Although the Senate acted favorably on the Slavery Convention, it has tabled the Conventions on the Political Rights of Women and the Abolition of Forced Labor. The reasons for not taking any action with respect to those two Conventions appear from the hearings to be a combination of three points of view: the Conventions apply to relations between a state and its own nationals, which is a matter of domestic concern; the proposals involved may conflict with specific constitutional guarantees; and they might override state laws in matters which are believed to be reserved to the states. The validity of these assertions has been debated hotly; Ambassador Goldberg, for example, strongly contested their soundness in hearings before the Senate Foreign Relations Committee.

Perhaps both Russia, which has also ratified the Supplemental Slavery Convention without reservation, and the United States believe that enforcement proceedings applied to them under Convention are highly unlikely. But in any event, there appears to be no appreciable slackening in their traditional stances. Unlike their activities in so many other areas, the two Great Powers have failed to take the initiative in trying to establish viable enforcement machinery on some international basis — bilateral, regional, or on a broader level.

The United States and the Soviets have engaged in great rivalry. We are both spending fortunes trying to see who will be the first to get a man on the moon.

Outer Space is a vitally important area; and I do not belittle it. But the Inner Space of this planet where most of us will live deserves priority. It is here we need pace-setters on how to make the earth a healthy place — where the land, air, and water remain unpolluted, where societies of abundance are designed, and where men of all tastes, creeds, and color can enjoy equal justice and can speak, write, paint, compose, and dance to suit their tastes.

We in the United States do not hesitate to use our great power to obtain vast material concessions. We indeed helped depose Mossadegh in Iran in exchange for 40 per cent of the oil consortium in which prior thereto we did not share. Why do we also use our power to gain "freedom" for the oppressed? Why do we recognize a Fascist regime in Greece before obtaining full amnesty for all persons arrested by the new government? Our insistence would be all that was necessary, because the new Greek regime could not possibly last without our support.

Competition between the Great Powers at this level would revolutionize the world and set the feet of all people on the path that truly leads to unity amidst the great diversities of religion, race, custom, language, and ideologies.

Seeing the absence of constructive initiative on the part of the Great Powers in the field of human rights, the other nations assume mostly a negative or neutral position. They may pass laws or amend constitutions so as verbally to comply with the Universal Declaration, but they continue in their old ways, making unequal justice and arbitrary arrests the order of the day. This has led many, who have worked long and hard at the UN on problems of human rights, to become disheartened and discouraged.

But voices of protest are still heard. Individuals in each nation are pressing for changes in attitudes and for reforms. Those voices are coming mostly from the smaller nations. And as the years pass and the European Commission of Human Rights and its associated Court record achievements and progress, the hope of men is strengthened.

Kotaro Tanaka, formerly Chief Justice of the Supreme Court of Japan and member of the International Court of Justice, recently urged that there be no vacuum in the protection of fundamental human rights and to that end proposed the machinery for world habeas corpus. Will jurists around the world follow his lead?

We have had as a human race rather vast experience in the use of *ad hoc* international agencies to settle problems between conflicting nations. These agencies have rendered thousands of decisions and it appears that the losing party very seldom has refused voluntarily to follow the award. The unification of mankind under a rule of law may be long in coming. On the other hand the advent of the atomic bomb, the growth of technology, the crying needs of underdeveloped nations, the desperate demands for revolutionary schemes that will get rid of the oppressive *status quo* that controls most of the world may well mean that international cooperative schemes will be faster in coming than we have imagined.

The human family is probably more closely knit today than ever before. The blacks, the yellows, the browns, and the whites are all coming to be more and more interdependent. Hunger once was the sole common denominator. Human dignity and fair treatment have now broadened the base of international concern. This has occurred in spite of clashing political ideologies. It makes ripe opportunities for experiments as challenging as an international writ of habeas corpus.

Chapter III

Trade and Aid
and the Developing Nations

The economic plight of the developing nations is extremely severe. Those with oil resources can, theoretically at least, convert them into factories, public housing, hospitals, schools, and the like. Most developing nations, however, are impoverished, having few natural resources except soil and people. The soil has not yet been opened up to scientific farming; the industrial plants are infants; and the people are not yet trained to the new tasks. The development of the new nations requires both capital and technical help. If they are to receive those kinds of aid in regular and sufficient amounts to transform their societies, the industrialized nations must establish somewhat the kind of relationship with them that we have with Appalachia and Harlem. Forms of federalism are, in other words, necessary if we are to have a viable world rather than one torn asunder by strife between the Rich and the Poor.

Trade

Most of the discussions of NATO presuppose a continuation both of the Cold War and the Rule of Force. In that posture the future of NATO would be resolved in essentially defensive terms: should the defense of Europe be left to its nations or in partnership with the United States; to what extent should West Germany be turned loose; what military arrangements can be made without the support of France; and the like.

But the idea of the Rule of Force which dominates our thinking is obsolete in terms of human survival. Two authors, speaking of

NATO, recently said, "While it is true that nothing is so powerful as an idea whose time has come, there is a corollary, that nothing is so weak as an idea whose time is past." The idea that the future of the world is secure in the old balance-of-power theory is "an idea whose time is past." In light of the growing membership in the nuclear club, survival calls for a radically different approach.

We still live with the old myths of American power and relish the alleged way in which Teddy Roosevelt handled the crisis over Venezuela in 1902-1903 when the German and British fleets lay off her coast, presumably to make landings to rectify damage done German and British interests in that country. The story is that Teddy Roosevelt gave the German ambassador word that, unless the claims were submitted to arbitration in twenty-four hours, he would send Dewey and the American fleet against them. Those are exciting stories of Americana. But they do not state the theme relevant to the needs of this nuclear age.

NATO, signed April 4, 1949, is a product of the Cold War. While the member states opt for "the freedom, common heritage and civilization of their peoples, founded on the principles of democracy, individual liberty and the rule of law," NATO's stance is primarily military. It is a defensive bloc against the Soviet Union. Its counterpart is the Warsaw Convention.

In the decade ending in 1960, we spent about one and a quarter billion dollars on NATO. The annual amount has increased since 1964, adding up to nearly $133 million in 1967. Most of this was for essentially military activities, although some was used to finance conferences between legislative representatives of member governments to discuss "common problems in the interest of the maintenance of peace and security in the North Atlantic area."

Although the original NATO agreement could expire in 1969 at the option of the parties, it appears at this writing that although outmoded, cut in two by France, and probably incapable of stopping any large conventional military attack, at least without unleashing the horror of nuclear weapons, NATO will not disappear. The new strategy of "flexible nuclear response" to attack, based on the concept of delayed employment of tactical nuclear weapons if required, may shore up NATO's claim to be a "deterrent"; but it only emphasizes the continuation of the policies of the Cold War.

A regime of a Rule of Law has no room either for the military NATO or the military Warsaw Convention. I would include them in what President Johnson has called the "bitter legacy of World War II."

Some think that the future of NATO lies in a federation of the Western world. The idea that the United States should vote for Union Now has been incessant. That step would further the trend toward polarization along ideological lines — a World-War-II development that has brought the people of this planet to the edge of the nuclear incinerator.

By the 1940's, eastern Europe was locked behind the Iron Curtain. As we near the seventies, almost every nation in that bloc is expressing in some form or other a degree of independence from Moscow. And western Europe is expressing in varied ways its independence of the United States. The time is ripe for the Great Powers to deal with NATO and the Warsaw Convention. The question is not what should be done unilaterally but rather what these two alliances would be worth in an exchange of a Rule of Force for a Rule of Law.

A regime of a Rule of Law would either dissolve these entities or transform them into vehicles to serve peaceful ends. One of the most useful would be their dedication to building arteries of commerce between East and West.

The Great Common Market, which we, starting with John Marshall, designed, levels trade barriers between our States, strikes down taxes that discriminate against interstate commerce, and the like — all with the aim of keeping the interstate arteries open and free from local restraints.

We cannot expect the same pattern at the world level without a unitary regime. But regional common markets offer opportunities that weave webs of commerce. And these commercial ties are partial foundations for coexistence.

The idea of a Common Market is rather commonplace these days. Wherever one goes, whether Africa, Latin America, Asia, the Middle East, or eastern Europe, there is always one in existence, or in embryonic form, or in some promotional stage. Every Common Market of course produces "a new legal order," to borrow a phrase from the Court of Justice of the European Community.

The Middle East is a logical place to start, as Premier Levi Eshkol has said many times. Israel is a natural market for Middle East fruits and for Middle East meat. The Middle East is a natural market for Israeli products. Trade heals wounds. It supplies therapy and seldom causes disorders.

The European Economic Community, which was created by the Treaty of Rome, is a true supranational government. The administrative arm is the European Commission, whose members are expected to act completely independent of their own national interest, and to adopt a European posture. They are not required either to seek or accept instructions from any government, and the governments who are signatories to the treaty agree that this provision will be observed. Their loyalty therefore is European. The Commission has the power to bring member states before the Court, if it decides that provisions of the treaty are not being honored. It formulates policies, and makes recommendations to the Council of Ministers which sits above it. Together with the Council of Ministers, it performs legislative functions.

The Council of Ministers represents the member states; the ministers act on a national rather than a supranational basis. But in order for the supranational principle to be a reality, the decisions of the Council are taken by a majority vote, unanimity not being required.

There is, in addition, the European Parliament, which in fact has no legislative function. It is purely consultative, with the exception that it has the power to dismiss the Commission as a body by a vote of censorship, carried by a two-thirds majority. Even so, the members of the Commission remain in office until they are replaced, and the replacement must be by the unanimous agreement of the governments of the member states. In practice, the relations between the Commission and the Parliament have been excellent.

If there is conflict within the European Community, it is between the Council and the Parliament. Each is concerned with political decisions, and the national interests do collide at times.

The crises have been numerous, one of the most acute relating to agriculture. In Germany prices are high; in France, they are comparatively low. Real integration of the economies of the two would give France a large market in Germany. Moreover, if France exported outside the community, she would be entitled to large deficiency payments from the other members. There has also been the question of who should administer the revenues charged on imports from outside countries — the Community or the several member states. In spite of these conflicts where a national interest often opposes the supranational one, the organization has survived.

The other agency of the Community is the Court of Justice, which again is supranational in character. Cases are brought before the

Court on reference by the Commission, and while the decisions have not been numerous, they have been very important in ensuring that the obligations of the states have been carried out. As of 1967, none of the decisions of the Court has been defied, all of them having been carried out. The Court consists of seven judges appointed for terms of six years, again by unanimous agreement of the member states. They must be law-trained and qualified to hold the highest judicial office in their home state, or otherwise be possessed of outstanding qualifications. The Court has jurisdiction not only respecting the member states, but also respecting the claims of individuals for damage actions and civil suits to review fines imposed by various organs of the Community. It has a rule that bars all dissenting opinions, each decision of the Court being *per curiam,* i.e., anonymous, no dissents being written or even recorded. That policy is designed to further the atmosphere of unity rather than division.

The European Common Market is in a real sense a new form of federalism, and that type of federalism will in time be found highly useful in many diverse situations around the world, trade being a prime example.

A significant development took place in East Africa in 1967. Throughout parts of Africa the tendency has been toward pulverization of countries due primarily to ancient animosities between tribes. Nigeria is a prime example, the Ibo tribe splitting off the eastern region and calling itself an independent nation, Biafra. The opposite trend appeared in East Africa when Kenya, Tanzania, and Uganda signed the Treaty for East African Cooperation, effective December 1, 1967.

The treaty is an ambitious start toward (1) building a common market, (2) economic planning, (3) operation of universities serving the three nations, (4) coordination of transport policy, (5) creation of an East African Development Bank.

The Treaty creates various executive agencies, a legislative assembly, and a Court of Appeal for East Africa. What form of federalism will emerge cannot be predicted. But the spirit of cooperation is so strong that East Africa may well produce in time a federal regime that surpasses the EEC.

The East Africa Common Services Organization, formed in 1961, was a start toward a form of federalism. It made the Court of Appeal for East Africa a regional court of appellate jurisdiction in criminal and civil cases. This court, whose antecedents trace to 1902, survived the grant of independence and became probably the most active agency in EACSO. Though EACSO was abrogated by the Treaty for East African Cooperation, June 6, 1967, the Court of Appeals was continued and in fact "deemed to have been established" by the Treaty.

The Caribbean Free Trade Association was established in 1965 by the governments of Antigua, Barbados, and Guyana (formerly British Guiana). Its purpose is to broaden domestic markets through the elimination of trade barriers between the member territories or states, and the treaty envisages the eventual creation of a customs union and viable economic community for all Caribbean countries. The institutions of the Association are a Council (composed of a representative of each member country, with one vote) and "such organs as the Council may set up." The Association is more similar to the European Free Trade Association, which will be discussed later, than to the European Common Market; for at present there is no common external tariff imposed against nonmember countries.

The agreement provides for the elimination of import duties among member countries — some progressively, others immediately. Duties and quantitative restrictions against exports destined for member countries are proscribed. So are quantitative restrictions against imports from member countries, although in certain cases, such as balance of payments difficulties or a substantial increase in unemployment due to a decrease in internal demand for a domestic product, it is provided that a member country may introduce quantitative restrictions on imports to solve its difficulties, upon notification to the Council. Certain restrictive business practices and types of government aid are also forbidden.

An enforcement procedure is established in the Treaty whereby, if one member country believes that another is violating the Treaty or that any benefit conferred upon it by the agreement is being frustrated, it may refer the matter to the Council if no agreement can be reached between the countries concerned. The Council may, by majority vote, examine the matter or refer the claim to an examining committee; and may make to any member country such recommendations as it deems necessary. If the Council has determined that there has been a violation of the Treaty, and the member country concerned has failed to comply with the Council's recommendations, the Council may, by majority vote, authorize any member country to suspend the application of certain obligations under the Treaty with respect to the member country which has not complied.

These hopeful signs for cooperation among the developing countries point out, however, the difficult trade problems which they face. There is a general lack of consensus and unity among developing countries, which becomes evident at international conferences and in the history of commodity agreements. While generalizations have validity when one is comparing the poor with the rich, they often give a stereotyped and unreal picture of the less-developed countries. There is great diversity in the developing world.

Perhaps the most striking variation is in size. The typical poor country is small, with not more than ten million inhabitants, though the list of poor countries also includes the world's largest non-Communist country, India. Moreover, Brazil, India, Indonesia, Mexico, Nigeria, and Pakistan contain over 50 per cent of the population of the developing world. Thus, although the typical developing country is small, the typical inhabitant of the developing world lives in a large nation.

The less-developed countries as a whole have had little share in the expansion of world trade. Thus, from 1954 to 1965, while exports from developed countries increased by 140 per cent, exports from less-developed countries rose by only 60 per cent.

Moreover, while the price index of exports from developed areas to underdeveloped areas during the same period rose from 94 to 104 points, the price index of exports from underdeveloped areas to developed areas declined during that period from 105 to 98 points. Thus terms of trade (that is, the export price index divided by the import price index) of developing to developed nations declined from 112 to 93. The export price index of the developing nations reflected a sharp price fall in the primary commodities of food, beverages, tobacco, and fuel. The rise of the export price index of developed nations was due to a price increase in machinery and other manufactures.

Moreover, the composition of exports of the less-developed countries shows clearly the preponderance of primary commodities — generally, food, beverages, tobacco, agricultural raw materials, mineral oils, and fuel. Although manufactures, including refined ores, have been and will be the most dynamic element of world exports, they accounted in 1965 for only 18 per cent of less-developed countries' exports. Another variation among developing countries is the ratio of exports to GNP. All developing countries are heavily dependent on exports, some more so than others.

When world demand for primary products slackens and/or the terms of trade of developing countries worsen, countries with a high export ratio are most affected by such changes. Not only does it mean a decrease in foreign exchange, which enables a developing country to finance the import of capital goods and industrial raw materials for economic growth; it also affects the income of those working for export production.

The present ratio of exports to GNP seems closely allied to size. Those countries which are heavily dependent on exports for income are mostly quite small. Trinidad (1 million people) is an extreme case, exporting 76 per cent of her GNP. Israel (2.6 million) has exported up to 40 per cent of her GNP. Bolivia (3.7 million), Burma (24.7 million), Ceylon (11.2 million), Ghana (7.7 million), Togo (1.7 million), Morocco (13.3 million) and Tunisia (4.4 million), exporting 21 per cent, 18 per cent, 26 per cent, 16 per cent, 23 per cent, 20 per cent and 20 per cent respectively, are more typical of those countries which export a substantial proportion of their GNP.

India, Indonesia, Pakistan, and Brazil — the largest countries, and the first three also the poorest — export only between 6 per cent and 9 per cent of their respective GNP. These countries are less dependent on exports and therefore less vulnerable to fluctuations in world demand for primary products and to unfavorable development in terms of trade. Yet in order to overcome their extreme poverty and to achieve sustained economic growth despite population explosion, they need capital goods and industrial raw materials which they have to import and which they must finance.

The cost of new industries in developing countries is often excessive because of the relative smallness of the national market. It is difficult, therefore, to increase exports because production costs are high; those costs are high because of the difficulty of realizing economies of scale in the absence of exports.

The balance of payments owed by the developing countries is greatly affected by the exports and imports of services, particularly those related to transportation. In 1961 there was an unfavorable balance of nearly $2 billion on the transport account, which represents nearly 35 per cent of the total unfavorable balance for goods and services combined, i.e., $5.25 billion.

The Atlantic countries take 60 per cent of the manufactured exports from developing nations, the United States buying the most. But the total of these manufactured exports are less than 4 per cent of the imports of the developed nations.

The exports of manufactures by developing nations (exclusive of refined nonprecious metals) constitute only about 10 per cent of their exports and only about 4 per cent of world exports of manufactured goods. Yet the developing nations buy nearly one-fourth of the manufactured products entering world trade.

Asia is the leading exporter of manufactured products among the underdeveloped countries, and by quite a large margin — about 50 per cent if metals are included, and 75 per cent if they are not. Total Asian manufactured exports are, of course, still small — amounting in 1964 to $2.7 billion, compared to $80.8 billion for the industrialized countries (excluding the Soviet Union). And total manufactured exports from underdeveloped countries represent only about 10 per cent of their total exports, and 4 per cent of world exports. The manufactured export trade is also highly specialized, primarily concentrated on light products with a high labor content or on processing of domestic raw materials. Moreover, manufacturing is highly concentrated — in 1963 over half of the toal exports of less developed countries originated in four countries (India, Israel, Mexico, and Hong Kong); while the nine top exporters accounted for about 70 per cent of the total manufactured exports of underdeveloped countries.

Because world trade in manufactured products has grown rapidly and promises to maintain that trend, the less developed countries tend to regard industrialization as the quickest route to development; but stiff resistance to such an approach is maintained by high tariff walls and other restrictive trade policies of the developed countries. Thus, textile products are subject to some kind of import restrictions in more countries than most other items. The comparatively more liberal treatment of imports other than textiles is due to the fact that the value of that trade is generally small. Efforts were made in the late 1950's to adjust the import controls over cotton textiles, and various developed and developing countries entered into long-term arrangements of that character. But these arrangements had escape clauses. For example, the importing nation that unilaterally claimed a condition of market disruption had in its hands the weapon for discrimination against developing countries; and that weapon was used without any international review.

In any event, it appears that at present only a few of the less developed countries are capable of turning more and more to manufactures to increase export earnings; the rest must continue to rely on developing increased commodity exports.

This has two main implications with respect to relations among the developing states themselves. First, agricultural products of large regions tend to be similar. The transportation system between underdeveloped areas is inadequate and often nonexistent. Historically the less developed countries have been oriented in their trade patterns toward the developed world. The result is that trade with one another remains very small. Second, the developing countries often have conflicting interests. There are at present eighteen African countries associated with the European Common Market. They have no concern that other underedeveloped nations should share the same advantages. The developing nations have not as yet developed an overall consensus. In some areas trade restrictions in one developing country affect another developing country. The less developed country which might be called "rich" may be unwilling to permit preferential treatment to a "poor" developing country. Third, the range of commodities which comprise the bulk of world exports in primary products is fairly narrow. One or two commodities often account for more than 50 per cent of the total export of a given country.

The future seems bleak for most developing countries if their main reliance is on commodity trade. The powerful desire to industrialize quickly stems not only from the close relation between industrialization and economic development but also from the desire to obtain foreign exchange as a result of exports. The value of world exports of manufactured articles increased at the rate of 8.1 per cent annually from 1955 to 1963 as compared with a rate of 3.1 per cent for commodities. Trade in manufactured goods appears therefore to be the way in which to obtain rapid increases in export goods and foreign exchange.

In addition to the slow growth rate of commodity trade, as compared to trade in manufactured articles, prospects for trade in commodities vary greatly, both by product and by country. For example, Latin America is the major food and beverage exporter, while the Middle East is the major oil exporter. Because most Latin American countries specialize in exporting products with fairly low elasticities of demand, and due to great increases in population along with inflationary tendencies, Latin America's prospects for increasing exports in commodities are poor. In the Middle East, where oil exports account for about 75 per cent of all regional exports, all but the major oil producing countries face problems, particularly since commoditity exports in each country are not greatly diversified. On the other hand, Africa, because of its low production costs and abundant supplies, is in a relatively strong position to increase its commodity exports, at the expense of other less developed regions. But Asia, faced with burgeoning populations and the competing pressure of synthetic materials by importing countries, faces large problems. For example, synthetics compete strongly with rubber products; and the principal clients of rice exporters are other less developed countries.

While the developing countries, except for Israel and Hong Kong, are first and foremost exporters of primary products, they all face different problems according to their specific export commodities and their geographical location.

The factors which influence markets for primary products (and the countries which trade in them) vary enormously from one commodity to another. There are three groups of commodities:

Foodstuffs, for which world demand is likely to increase more slowly than demand for other goods;

Agricultural raw materials, for which demand is derived from the demand of manufactured goods and which are likely to continue to suffer from severe fluctuations in demand and increasing competition from synthetic substitutes (e.g., rubber and nitrates);

Minerals, demand for which will probably remain fairly buoyant though fluctuations are likely for the same reasons that affect agricultural raw materials.

Even within these categories, however, producers of different commodities will probably face quite different problems. The prospect for exports of coffee from poor countries, for example, is better than for sugar, because no close substitute is likely to be produced outside the tropics. The class of minerals contains both tin (which has suffered from severe price fluctuations since the war and a demand which has increased very little in the last fifty years) and petroleum (whose price has fluctuated very little even by comparison with manufactures, the world consumption of which has increased nearly forty times in the last fifty years).

Although the recent Kennedy Round received a great deal of publicity, it rendered little assistance to the less developed nations. The tariff agreements at the Kennedy Round will substantially affect trade — worth $40 billion a year — but mostly between industrialized countries. In general, the negotiations are only of slight interest to the less developed countries. The list of products exempted from the tariff negotiations covered one-fourth of trade in manufactures, including textiles and many other products of interest to developing nations. Thus, the exemption list represents probably a serious source of discrimination against products from those countries. In addition, although it was agreed during the negotiations that industrialized nations would not expect full reciprocity from less developed countries when bargaining for trade cuts, this did not mean that the latter would be authorized to erect new trade barriers to protect their infant industries. Nor did it mean preferential treatment for their products. Moreover, nothing was done to ease quota restrictions on products vital to the trade of developing countries; nor was anything done to stabilize prices of primary commodities. Finally, the few tariff cuts in which the less developed countries are interested will be implemented in five annual stages. The whole benefit from the tariff cuts will therefore be felt only in 1973; although there is still hope that the industrialized countries will take the necessary steps to grant the tariff-cut benefits to less developed nations at an earlier date.

There were, however, at least two favorable aspects of the Kennedy Round for the less-developed countries, in addition to the agreement by industrialized nations not to expect full reciprocity in tariff cuts. New antidumping rules agreed upon earlier in the Kennedy Round will stop rich countries from imposing special tariff restrictions on goods from low-wage countries. And a world-grains agreement was successfully negotiated that guarantees higher minimum world trading prices, with commitments from the industrial powers to provide for food aid to less developed countries. But, despite the Kennedy Round, significant trade barriers still face the developing countries.

The United States has very few tariffs on imported raw materials; the European countries have somewhat more. Tariffs, quotas, and non-tariff/non-quota barriers are mainly applied to processed products. This is an old warhorse of the mercantile system which never disappeared from the trade politics of the developed world.

Although industrialized countries point out that their tariffs on manufactures are already quite low (around 12 per cent for the

United States and the Common Market), a presentation of average tariffs distorts the true picture. First, effective rates of protection are higher than the nominal tariff rates imply. For example, before the Kennedy Round the Common Market tariff was zero on hides and skins, 9 per cent on leather, and 16 per cent on leather products. These rates obviously would discourage the setting up of leather industries in developing countries. Assuming an added value of 50 per cent in turning skins into leather goods, the Common Market tariff of 16 per cent should really be viewed as the protection given to domestic producers for adding value to skins and turning them into leather manufactures. In other words, the producer of leather manufactures in a developing country is faced with a 16 per cent tariff not on leather manufactures as such, but on the 50 per cent of the value added; and the effective tariff is 32 per cent.

Second, developing countries export only a few manufactured items, so that the general level of tariffs gives no indication of the discrimination against them with respect to their particular products.

Finally, a number of export countries with relatively low tariff levels use quantitative controls and non-tariff/non-quota barriers to prevent entry of manufactured goods from developing countries. It is therefore misleading to draw attention to average tariff levels, nominal or effective, as the sole criterion of discrimination against developing nations. While a moderate tariff wall can be scaled by an increase in efficiency, many of the non-tariff barriers cannot be surmounted at all, or can be overcome only with great difficulty.

The General Agreement on Tariffs and Trade (GATT), under whose auspices the Kennedy Round was held, does not offer much promise for developing countries. That agreement was formed in the postwar period by the developed countries; and it has resulted in the lowering of trade barriers in successive rounds since 1948. But like the Universal Declaration of Human Rights, GATT is in some respects out of touch with the needs of the less-developed countries. Although since 1965 GATT has been increasingly concerned with the trade problems of developing countries, and has encouraged the lowering of duties on certain products of principal export interest to those countries, the lack of any truly significant positive measure during the Kennedy Round — apart from the agreement of the industrialized nations not to expect full reciprocity, in contrast to the general GATT policy — decreases the chances that GATT will provide an imaginative, creative force in this area.

Apart from GATT, the problems of developing countries with respect to world trade cannot be assessed accurately without taking account of the activities of other international trade groupings — specifically, the European Free Trade Association (EFTA), and the European Economic Community (EEC).

The European Free Trade Association was established in 1960 to expand economic activity and trade in and among the areas covered by the Association. At present seven countries are members of the Association — Austria, Denmark, Norway, Portugal, Sweden, Switzerland, and the United Kingdom. Finland is an Associate Member.

Fair competition in trade between member states was a primary object of the Association; in particular, elimination of tariff, quota, and other trade restrictions between member states was envisaged. And, by the end of 1966, the establishment of a free trade area was largely realized for industrial products. After December 31, 1966, there were no longer any import duties imposed by the member states on industrial goods traded within the Association, except for a very few items. Finland was to have eliminated its import duties by the end of 1967. Norway will retain a very few tariffs until 1969; Portugal, because of its less-developed condition, will follow a slower schedule of tariff removal. But in essence, we now have the world's first free trade area in industrial goods.

Between 1959, the year prior to the beginning of tariff cuts, and 1966, the year of completion of tariff removal for most countries in EFTA, trade between the eight EFTA countries increased by 112 per cent. The yearly growth rate was therefore 11.4 per cent, compared to a rate of about 5.5 per cent in the six years preceding 1959; so it is clear that trade relations among member states have improved considerably.

EFTA trade with countries other than the United States or members of the European Economic Community has generally increased since 1959, but more slowly than that with America or the Common Market countries. The 1966 figures are revealing. Total exports to the United States increased by 22.5 per cent, while total imports from the United States increased by 7 per cent; exports to the EEC countries increased by 4.4 per cent, while imports increased by 5.6 per cent. With respect to the rest of the world, however, total EFTA exports increased by 4.9 per cent but imports increased by only 2.2 per cent. The breakdown of imports from countries other than the United States and EEC states is not available for 1966, but the low growth rate of imports suggests that underdeveloped countries are not faced with a particularly favorable market among EFTA countries. In absolute terms, countries other than the United States or members of EFTA or the EEC accounted in 1966 for over $13 billion of EFTA imports. Imports from member EFTA countries totaled almost $8 billion; those from EEC states amounted to over $11 billion; and imports from the United States totaled about $3.5 billion.

In 1965, for which a breakdown by country is available, trade with less developed countries represented less than 18 per cent of total EFTA trade, and only about 14 per cent of the total trade of the less developed countries. The United Kingdom, of course, was the major EFTA trader with underdeveloped countries; the latter accounted for more than 25 per cent of total British trade, and trade with the United Kingdom amounted to about 10 per cent of the total trade of underdeveloped countries. But the share of the developing countries in the total trade of the other EFTA states is quite small. At the same time, there is a relatively large deficit in total EFTA trade with underdeveloped countries, due to the sizeable deficit of the United Kingdom, which is not overcome by the surplus of the other EFTA states.

As is true for the rest of the developed world, manufactured goods represent the major exports from EFTA states to less developed countries — about 85 per cent of total exports to those states — while primary commodities account for most of the EFTA imports from developing nations, oil and oil products representing a large portion. Geographically, trade is concentrated with underdeveloped countries located in the Commonwealth and overseas Portuguese areas. For countries other than the United Kingdom and Portugal, Latin America is the major supplier of imports; and is generally the major recipient of exports.

Unlike the Rome Treaty, the EFTA Convention did not attempt to change member countries' trade relations with third countries. Consequently, there is no common external tariff, and the tariffs of each member state on third country goods, including those from developing countries, remain unaffected by the Convention. Although the Common Market states have associated certain African countries with the European Community, thus giving them preferential treatment in a wider market, this has not been done by EFTA, even for the less-developed countries in the Commonwealth or Portuguese overseas areas.

In July, 1963, the EEC countries and seventeen African states plus Madagascar signed the Yaounde Convention designed to promote an increase in trade between the latter countries, known as the Associated African States and Madagascar (AASM), and EEC states. The 1963 Convention of Association gave more meaningful content to the earlier declaration of the EEC countries in the Treaty of Rome concerning their relations with certain overseas countries or territories.

With respect to trade, the Yaounde Convention provided that there should be created a "zone of free movement for goods adapted to the necessities of those economies which are not yet sufficiently industralised." In practice, this means three things:

(a) the Associated States have free access to the Common Market, and in return must open their markets to products from EEC states;

(b) the Associated States are permitted (by an express provision of the Convention) to adopt measures to protect their growing economies and infant industries;

(c) the Associated States are free, within quite flexible limits, to participate in the maintenance or establishment of customs unions or free-trade areas among the Associated States or with one or more third countries.

Using the first nine months of 1964, 1965, and 1966 as a comparative basis, total imports from AASM countries to EEC states increased by about 16 per cent between 1964 and 1966, while total exports from EEC countries to the Associated States increased only at about one third that rate. The EEC balance with the AASM has always shown a deficit, which increased substantially between 1964 and 1966. Total EEC/AASM trade (imports plus exports) increased about 11.6 per cent between 1964 and 1966, the major portion of that increase occurring between 1965 and 1966.

The preferential treatment which these Associated States receive within the Common Market has certain effects on overall trade patterns for underdeveloped countries. Any system of preferences which includes less than all developing countries favors some at the expense of others. Uneven advantages are created, and in a sense, the poor are aligned against the poor. In many areas, for example, trade restrictions of developing nations affect other less developed countries to a great extent. Resistance to cooperation among all developing states may well be increased by absorption of some into advantageous trading blocs, such as the EEC. Among the developing countries themselves, then, there is much room for cooperation.

Aid

Every developing nation I have visited wants to follow in the steps of the Great Powers and industrialize. As Nehru put it: "There are no developed and underdeveloped countries; there are countries which are industrialized and those which are not." There is wisdom in that observation, for our ghettos are living testimony that the United States is in some respects underdeveloped. For industrialization to proceed successfully, capital accumulation is the first problem, whether private capitalism or state capitalism. We solved that initial problem before 1860. We borrowed for canals, railroads, turnpikes, and other public projects, obtaining most of our capital from Europe. Discovery of gold was important in creating bank credit that helped finance business activity.

Soviet Russia solved the problem of capital accumulation by 1940, taking the savings out of the hides of her people. Capital accumulation unlocked the doors to industrialization, for both nations had a vast reservoir of scientists and technicians.

Capital accumulation plus technological competence are in this age hardly enough to produce a viable society. Today's problem is to build an industrial system on a broad popular base, not to create an exploitive industrial oligarchy. Karl Marx thought this could not be done, saying that the state, being managed by "the bourgeoisie," would never consent to its transformation into an economic democracy. But the broadening of the electorate in England and the existence of the free franchise here enabled the people in time to catch up with the Robber Barons and through social legislation establish economies designed to safeguard both consumers and workers against injustices. The hypotheses on which Karl Marx wrote were therefore largely discredited by history.

In time the technology of both Russia and the Western world produced such abundance that it was easy to see how the machines of the rich could supply most of the material wants of the poor in whatever nation the poor lived. That has become a real spectre to some

developing nations. It is along these lines that many current international controversies proceed. The problem of the developing
country starts with the fear that it may become the drawer of water
and the hewer of wood for industry in the rich nation. That was the
nub of the 1948 crisis between Yugoslavia and the Soviet Union
which led to a break of relations. For the Yugoslavs wanted a higher
standard of living than one possible if their country merely supplied
the raw materials for the Soviet industrial plant and were the consumers of its products.

The industrial pattern of Africa and Latin America showed generally the movement of raw materials to the ports and from thence
to Europe and America. The local economy benefited from wages;
but the profits and capital gains went abroad. There were exceptions;
but this was the general pattern. Moreover, Western trading houses
poured Western goods into developing countries. This led, as in India and China, to the destruction of local handicrafts; and capital
that might have been accumulated by local manufacturers and traders was absorbed into the economies of the West, largely Europe.
This was one product of the colonial period; and it is also a product
of the new imperialism of all capitalistic regimes. It helps negate the
development of local industry and local markets in the developing
nations, making them suppliers of raw materials to the industrial
plants of the rich and making them also consumers of the products
of the existing machines of mass production. The extent and depth
of this development can be understood if it is remembered that Japan
— the only Asian country free of colonial rule or intervention —
was the first Asian nation to make an industrial breakthrough.

The second fear of developing nations is that even if they become
industrialized, they will be high-cost producers compared with the
developed nations and unable to compete in the same markets. In
addition to obtaining tariff preferences for their exports in the markets of the rich, they desire to erect trade barriers against imports.
First, they want to protect their infant industries. And second, they
want to convert imports of luxury nonessential goods to imports that
are sorely needed for their own industrial development.

Agriculture

The early preoccupation with industrialization has given way to a
priority for agriculture. Public health measures have been so success-

ful that population is burgeoning everywhere. India, which seventy years ago was exporting one million tons of wheat, experiences a deficit of food; and she imported ten million tons of foodgrams a year.

What was true of India was true of other developing nations. Until 1954 the developing nations in the free world exported nearly four million metric tons. Since 1955 they have become importers, the amount reaching 16.5 million metric tons in 1965.

In India, 55,000 babies are born every day. The annual net population increase is now 13 million. This means that agriculture now receives the priority.

The President's Science Advisory Committee reported in 1967 that if the world population continues to increase at the 1965 rates, 52 per cent more calories will be required by 1985. Even if the population increase drops 30 per cent from its present level, the caloric requirements will still be 43 per cent higher by 1985.

Without a drop in the population growth rate, India will require 108 per cent more calories by 1985. With a 30 per cent decrease, the caloric requirement will increase 88 per cent.

The same figures for Pakistan are 146 per cent and 118 per cent. For Brazil they are 104 per cent and 91 per cent.

Agriculture in India employs 140 million people or about 25 per cent of India's 510 million. About eight million or 4 per cent of our population take care of our food production. This suggests that India's agriculture has not yet gone through the vast technological revolution that has affected agriculture as well as industry in this nation and in Europe.

I was in Bhopal, a decade or so ago when Japanese rice experts were teaching Indian farmers new techniques. The result was an increase per unit of land of 1,000 per cent in rice production.

Out of India comes the news that as a result of seed selection and new hybrid strains, the yields of wheat, jowar, bajra, maize, groundnuts, linseed, grape seed, and mustard have increased between 70 per cent and 80 per cent and even more. Since the new hybrids are quick growing, two and even three crops are being realized — *where the land is irrigated.* In 1968 India produced a bumper crop of grain — a record 95,800,000 tons. New technology — fertilizers, pesticides, and high-yield seeds — was a prime factor. India was spending in 1968 about eight times more of its foreign exchange for fertilizers than it did in 1960, and domestic fertilizer factories were beginning to appear.

Out of a Ford & Rockefeller rice institute at Los Banos, Philippines, in 1967 came a new "miracle rice" that matures in 120 days rather than in 150, irrespective of the season. And it has shorter, sturdier stems with heavy heads that stand up well no matter the weather.

Multiple cropping has increased the need for mechanization. Tracts that could be harvested by two bullocks and three women in a week, provided there were enough wind to make separation of chaff possible, can be done in less than a day by machinery. If there were no wind, the crop might lie in the fields for six weeks or more, during which time the crop might be impaired by exposure to the weather.

A thrasher and tractor not only can do the job in less than a day but also have the new crop planted in the next day or so. And the cost of a thrasher and tractor can be recovered in a single season by hiring it out for a fee computed by what it would cost to do the job manually. These are the powerful forces behind the mechanization trend in India.

Other startling consequences could result in India. Today she produces less than one-quarter of the commercial fertilizers she needs for food production — 500,000 tons of nitrogen and 260,000 tons of phosphates. By 1972 she plans to be producing 2.2 million tons of nitrogen and 550,000 tons of phosphates. With fertilizers available, European and American agricultural methods could be employed; and if they were used, it is even possible that India could have a food surplus. The reason is that the acreage she farms is about equal to our own. Though her population is two and a half that of ours, we use our cereals to produce proteins, while India is largely vegetarian. If the three pounds of cereals we use to produce one pound of meat were available in the consumer market, we would have a tremendous surplus. India, the vegetarian nation, can approximate our present surplus, if she uses modern methods. Fertilizers are one key to that end; water is another.

India has plenty of water; the problem is to conserve it for year-around use and not trust the rains to produce annually the amount needed. The High Aswan Dam on the Nile has a capacity of 127 million acre-feet; the Kauba in Africa, 150 million acre-feet. Yet in spite of the fact that five hundred irrigation projects have been launched in the last fifteen years, India stores in reservoirs only 50 million acre-feet as against our 600 million acre-feet.

India is now shifting from dams to tube wells which go down three hundred feet and dug wells which go to forty feet. Tens of thousands of these wells have recently been drilled or dug. It has been discovered that the Gangetic Plain contains the largest underground reservoir in the world.

Where the Indian farmer has used modern agricultural methods, his net income per five acres of land has jumped from $67.10 to $400.65. With a new tube well he can get a second crop which will more than double that income.

The keys to the agricultural problems of most developing nations, then, start with water and commercial fertilizers — each of which requires application of modern technology and investment of large funds, and these usually implicate international agencies.

Beyond these aspects of modern agriculture is the problem of large-scale production — large enough to permit the use of machinery. The tendency among developing nations has been a pulverization of land ownership into extremely small parcels — much of it into uneconomic units. We of the West think of agricultural efficiency in terms of tractors and the like. Yet they say in India that one of its villages could live for a week on the wheat that an American or Canadian harvesting machine leaves behind. And when it comes to food grains the largest output per acre is not in the United States but in Japan and Taiwan, where the laws limit the size of farms to 7.5 acres and 10 acres respectively. The main role of mechanization on the farm is to save labor by reducing the number of people required to operate a single unit, and by cutting down the time needed for harvesting so that multiple cropping may be practiced.

As the feudal, landed estates were broken up, Russia turned to collective farms and to state farms. India, where in most states a single family is limited to thirty acres, has turned more and more to cooperatives. As of 1967 India had

—about 7,000 coops engaged in farming;
—3,000 cooperative marketing societies;
—several hundred cooperative sugar factories that produce about one-fourth of the total sugar output of India;
—over 150 cotton ginning and pressing coops;
—nearly 9,000 other types of processing coops.

Since feeding the poor is now an international problem, modernization of agriculture is likewise an international burden. Financing irrigation projects and commercial fertilizer plants is one facet of the problem. Financing cooperative farming, cooperative processing, co-operative marketing is another. This financing must be of an international character for two reasons:

(1) the poverty of the developing nations and the huge amount of funds required make it imperative;

(2) even in areas such as Latin America where there is a rich upper class, the existing instrumentalities of finance are as *underdeveloped* as the villages themselves. For it must be remembered that in an *underdeveloped* nation most phases of its life are *underdeveloped* — from the church to the bank to the village to medical care to farming.

Modernization of agriculture means the conversion of individual farmers to a commercial system in which production is primarily for distant markets, *viz.*, the modernization of marketing systems. For a nation to experience a technological revolution in agriculture, it must have available fertilizers, tools, high-yielding seeds, pest controls, irrigation waters, and many other articles and commodities. It was this area that marked a vast gap in the early efforts to modernize agriculture in Latin America. The American and European experts went down and told the farmers precisely what they had to do. But when they left there were none of the credit institutions available to enable the farmers to buy the tools and fertilizers and pest controls that they needed, and very often those articles were at distant points in a particular country or obtainable only overseas. This was the problem to which the Maryknoll Fathers addressed themselves when they realized the first ingredient of agricultural reform was the creation of a credit union.

The financial requirements of the technological agricultural revolution in the developing nations are enormous. The President's Science Advisory Committee estimates that when fertilizers, seeds, mechanization, and pesticides alone are considered, a 4 per cent growth rate in agriculture will require at the start $300 million annually, and by 1985, $4 billion annually. To achieve that growth rate, capital investments would have to increase $12 billion annually above the 1965 base.

International agencies — both those supplying financial help and technical assistance — are needed to modernize agriculture in the developing nations.

The World Bank group, up to the end of 1967, helped finance

some 112 agricultural projects with loans or credits for a total of $1.2 billion dollars. Some were flood-control projects and irrigation projects.

In Brazil, India, and Senegal important fertilizer projects have been established. Livestock improvement, mechanization, tree crop production, plantation development, fisheries, and forestry all have been aided.

In Tunisia a project was financed which transformed traditionally small subsistence holdings of peasants into larger viable production units. A like project undertaken in Kenya. Land resettlement projects have been financed.

Cooperatives in developing nations face difficulties because of an untrained management, a weak financial basis, and a limited scale of operation. Direct help through the cooperatives or their members is therefore often not feasible and various alternatives have been used. One is a public corporation with substantial autonomy which performs many functions of the cooperative, such as was done in Uganda with the Uganda Tea Growers' Corporation. The producers are represented on its Board. In time perhaps tea cooperatives will take the place of the public corporation.

The National Development Credit Agency of Tanzania is also an autonomous public authority to which credit is extended and which in turn finances cooperative processing and marketing groups.

In Uraguay, the World Bank Group is financing cooperative processing and cooperative marketing, the funds being channeled through the existing central-bank system. The whole project is supervised by a so-called Honorary Commission, which employs a staff of technicians to make certain of economic feasibility and efficiency of operation.

In Colombia, the World Bank Group is financing dairy production, the products being marketed through existing cooperative processing and marketing channels.

In Tunisia, production cooperatives are being financed by the World Bank Group and they act as single agents for marketing of the various products. The traditional small Tunisian farmers are being associated with modern estates formerly owned by French Colons, the cooperative being used to expand the application of modern and efficient large-scale farming operations.

Other production cooperatives in various parts of the underdeveloped world are seeking financing.

The United States Agency for International Development (AID)
is helping to train farmers for cooperative regimes, its most ambitious program being in Uganda.

AID is training farmers in improved agricultural practices in numerous countries, sometimes general education in production, sometimes specialized, as for example in wheat, hybrid corn, and the like.

What has been done to date is, of course, merely a token of the
kind of financial assistance that is needed. Important as are these
projects, they have some built-in limitations which are characteristic of
other aid projects for the developing countries which will be discussed later.

Industrialization

It is obvious that the development of agriculture and the development of an industrial economy must go hand-in-hand, for a burgeoning agricultural economy means there are increasingly prosperous
customers who can buy the farm products.

We start with agricultural nations who want to become transformed. If they are to become viable societies, they need:

(1) Accumulation of capital
(2) The acquisition of technical and managerial skills
(3) The production of political systems that will make a new
     industrial regime viable.

The industrial revolution, like the agricultural one, entails a vast
infusion of outside capital. Of course those developing nations which
have resources such as oil have no such problem. But most of the developing nations need outside capital in order to develop the industries which will make it possible for them to exploit their local resources.

Great Britain, during the fifty years preceding World War I, invested
about 4 per cent of her GNP each year in her colonies. From 1905-
1917 that percentage rose to 7 per cent. In the early years of the Marshall Plan — fiscal 1949 and 1950 — the United States spent about
2 per cent of its GNP in aid. We are now down to less than three-
quarters of 1 per cent of our current GNP. In Asia, in the Middle
East, and in Europe the common talk is that if the United States would
commit 1 per cent of its GNP each year, and if the other industrial-

ized nations would do the same, the problems of the developing countries would in time be solved. In fact, the United Nations General Assembly adopted the 1 per cent formula as the target for aid to developing countries during the UN Development Decade, 1960-1970. A second goal established by the General Assembly was an annual growth rate of 5 per cent or more in the national income of less developed countries. Achievement of these objectives, however, has not yet even been approached for most countries. Only a colossal effort in development will make those objectives come true by 1980, not to mention 1970.

For purposes of our discussion, the developing countries are

—all Africa with the exception of South Africa;
—all America with the exception of the United States and Canada;
—all Asia except the USSR and Japan;
—all Oceania except Australia and New Zealand;
—and in Europe, Albania, Bulgaria, Cyprus, Greece, Malta, Portugal, Spain, Turkey, and perhaps Yugoslavia.

These areas comprise about one hundred countries and fifty dependent territories. They share in common a very low per capita income in comparison with the developed countries. With the exception of Israel and Venezuela, all of them have a per capita GDP of less than $600 a year. (GDP is private consumption, plus public consumption, plus gross investments, plus exports minus imports of goods and services. GNP is GDP plus payments from abroad minus payments to abroad of dividends, interest, and cross-border wages.)

Sixty per cent of the total population of aid-receiving countries live in countries where per capita GNP is less than $100 a year.

The pressure to hasten economic development is tremendous. As already noted, the success of any effort to overcome poverty is endangered by the annual high growth rates of population, which during 1958 to 1964 ranged from 1.1 in Yugoslavia, to 2.3 in India, to 2.7 in Egypt, to 2.8 in Guinea, to 3 in Peru, to 3.1 in Brazil, to 3.2 in Colombia. Israel, despite her high per capita income and diversified export structure, is still a less-developed country. Although she has a very high rate of population growth due to immigration, she nevertheless ranked first among less developed countries in growth rate of per capita GDP (7.2) ranging from 2 per cent to 10 per cent. This success, which makes her a challenge to other developing countries, can be ascribed to the amount of aid and war reparations received, to the high education level of the Euro-American Jews, and to the fact that the increase in population through immigration has meant an additional resource of manpower instantly available to contribute to the production process.

This last advantage is not granted to the other developing countries where high growth rates in population are due to natural increase and therefore impose a heavy burden on the economy. Forty-five per cent of the population of developing countries live in countries where 40 per cent of the population is less than fifteen years old. This means that a large part of the population must be supported by the working population. The population explosion in the less developed world is due mainly to a decrease an infant mortality rates but is not accompanied by a substantial rise in life expectancy even at age fifteen. Economic development requires vast capital investments, including investments in education and training of skilled workers. With low life expectancy, however, the cost to the economy of educating and training people is very high, as these people over a long time do not contribute to the production process. Differences in life expectancy and age structure among various developing countries must therefore be taken into consideration when dealing with characteristics of underdeveloped countries.

An annual growth rate of per capita GDP above 7 per cent is recorded only by Israel, Peru, and Yugoslavia, and in 1967 by Kenya. At the other extreme are countries with an average rate of growth of less than 2.5 per cent, e.g., Argentina and Burma. It is most likely that Indonesia, for which no data are available, would also be listed in this group. Most less developed countries range between these extremes. But as the annual rate of population growth in these countries is around 2 per cent to 2.3 per cent, the increases in per capita income are very small. Brazil, India, Indonesia, Mexico, Nigeria, and Pakistan — the six largest countries of the non-Communist developing world — account for more than one-half of the population of the less developed world, excluding mainland China. Four of these six (except Brazil and Mexico) with 750 million people and a yearly per capita income of less than $100 have not succeeded in achieving higher growth rates in per capita income.

Raymond W. Goldsmith has estimated that our annual growth rate for the last 120 years has been at an average annual rate of 1⅝ per cent of the GNP. Prior to 1839, the annual average growth rate was probably less than 1 per cent. And, while the per capita GNP was about $400 in 1839, it was probably $200 in colonial America. We apparently experienced an upward trend when the transition from agriculture to industry (plus the advent of the railroads) took place shortly before 1839. These figures from our own experience do not suggest that the problem of the developing nation need also be for a like long term. But they do suggest that, although the power of a small difference in compound interest rates is great when operating over a long period, a low growth rate in a world that is fast filling with people can well mean tragedy and despair.

Harrison Brown recently posed the question of what it would take to achieve a rate of economic growth in the developing countries which is sufficiently rapid to enable the average person to feel that his economic lot is improving appreciably during the course of his lifetime. His conclusion was as follows:

> In quantitative terms this would mean at least something like a doubling of per capita gross national income in about 25 years. Taking into account the fact that populations in many of the poorer countries are now doubling in about 25 years, the gross national income would have to increase at the rate of about 5.5 per cent per year in order for the per capita income to double in 25 years. This is a substantially higher rate of growth than that which has been achieved by most developing nations on a sustained basis even with the levels of economic assistance currently available.

The economies of most developing countries are heavily dependent on agriculture for income and employment. India, Indonesia, Nigeria, and Pakistan have typically rural economies. Israel, one of the countries which will most probably cease to be in the less developed group in the not too distant future, is with her 10 per cent share of agriculture in GDP least dependent on agriculture for income, though not for foreign exchange. As for Trinidad Tobago, it is heavily engaged in mining (petroleum), so that its 10 per cent is not a sign of a high degree of industrialization.

Aid, as well as fair terms of trade, is in incessant demand.

Aid means several different things. First, as to official aid, the transfer of physical resources and services from developed to less developed countries by means of fund or commodity grants is pure aid. This type of aid does not involve a subsequent export of real resources from developing to developed countries, but constitutes a net addition to the resources available to the receiving country.

What is, however, by and large considered as official assistance embraces.

(a) bilateral grants, and grant-like contributions
(b) bilateral net lending, and
(c) contributions to multilateral agencies.

Apart from grants and grantlike contributions, such as food, the broader definition of aid comprises, with respect to the developing countries, a variety of loans extended at more-or-less lenient terms. The question, What kind of aid? is therefore fully as important as, How much?

Some measure aid in terms of the net goods and services made available to the recipients. Thus, our Food for Peace Program (which amounts to some 17 per cent of the $87.1 billion committed under the different economic aid programs in fiscal years 1945 through 1966) transferred resources to less developed countries and constituted, therefore, grantlike aid to the recipient countries. Some measure aid in terms of the cost to the taxpayer. Official statistics on United States aid, however, mix both concepts. The reasons for measuring both the cost of aid to the United States and the terms on which aid is extended are of a political nature and reflect the appropriation struggle in the Congress.

Since the 1960's, grants no longer make up the major part of our official aid; and among official loans, the Export-Import Bank loans constitute an ever-increasing part. These loans, tied to United States procurement, are repayable in dollars and carry nearly commercial-like interest rates. Development grants are not used to finance capital projects that directly earn foreign exchange.

While American loans are supposed to promote the private enterprise system in the recipient country, they are not supposed to develop industries whose products might compete with United States products. These restrictions on the use of United States official bilateral grants and loans often thwart the financing of worthwhile investment projects, which alternatively must be financed by international organizations or through loans or direct investments by private capital.

Since 1945 the policy-makers in the Executive Branch have considered trade and aid to be alternative techniques of state-craft. They have told Congress again and again that less aid would be required if American trade barriers were lowered. Congress, however, has been unreceptive to the argument. Tariff legislation has traditionally been considered a "domestic question" and has therefore been channeled through the House Ways and Means Committee and the Senate Finance Committee. Since aid legislation goes through other committees, it is difficult for the Executive Branch to demonstrate the intimate relation that exists between aid and trade policies. By ignoring this relation, Congress has saddled the Executive with two conflicting lines of policy: on the one hand, Congress has resisted attempts to lower American trade barriers and thus to help foreigners to earn dollars; on the other, Congress has insisted on increasing foreign aid in the form of loans. The question then becomes: "How are foreigners going to acquire dollars to repay U. S. loans?"

A $128 billion figure is often given to aid extended from 1946 through June 30, 1967, but that embraces obligations or loan authorizations, that is to say aid committed and not aid disbursed. The computation is on a gross basis, repayments and interests not being taken into account.

That figure is approximately correct.

	Assistance (billions)		
	Economic	Military	Total
1. 1946–June 30, 1965	81.443	34.647	116.090
2. 1966 (fiscal)	5.616	1.258	6.874
3. 1946–June 30, 1966	87.059	35.905	122.965
ESTIMATES			
4. 1967 (fiscal)	4.441	.995	5.436
5. 1946–June 30, 1967	91.5	36.9	128.4

The data given as formal military aid do not cover the whole extent of military assistance extended to foreign countries:

First, payments for United States troops stationed in foreign countries are not included; they enter the United States Balance-of-

Payments account in somewhat the same manner as American tour-
ist expenditures. Second, the history of military assistance to Latin
American countries reveals that deliveries of tanks, destroyers, and
heavy equipment are considered as military assistance, while jeeps,
communication gears, engineering equipment, small arms, etc., which
are delivered to these countries to ensure internal security against
guerrilla-type activities, are not.

Yet the incomplete coverage of formal military assistance is somewhat offset by the overpricing of military deliveries, which tends to
exaggerate the amount of military aid.

United States economic assistance started in fiscal year 1949 with
the Marshall Plan and has included

—technical cooperation/development grants (including Alliance for
Progress grants);
—development loans (including Alliance for Progress loans);
—defense support/supporting assistance; and
—other assistance, including mainly contributions to International
Organization and Contingency Fund aid.

From fiscal year 1949 through fiscal year 1966, $42.6 billion were
committed, though only $38.4 billion were expended.

The following table shows the distribution of *aid* between Europe,
non-regional, and all other countries (mainly developing countries)
on the one hand, and between *grants* and *loans* on the other hand.

	Grants (1)	Loans (2)	Total (1) + (2)	Of Which Supporting Assistance	
				Grants	Loans
Total	31.5	11.1	42.6	24.5	3.3
Europe	13.4	1.8	15.2	13.2	1.7
Non-Regional	2.8	(*)	2.8	(*)	(*)
All other Countries ...	15.3	9.3	24.6	11.3	1.6

* Less than $50,000.

Supporting Assistance was called Defense Support through fiscal
year 1961 and was invented in the 1950's as a means of disguising

economic aid in order to make it more palatable to Congress. As for the 1960's, Supporting Assistance is clearly connected with military assistance. It is obvious that a large part of the so-called economic aid to the group of "all other countries" was in fact disguised military aid. Since 1960, fourteen countries have been dropped from the list of countries receiving Supporting Assistance. Still on the list in fiscal years 1965-1966 were Vietnam, Laos, Korea, and Jordan which received 88 per cent of the total Supporting Assistance, and half a dozen other countries. As for Latin America, besides Supporting Assistance, part of the Alliance for Progress aid has military character.

There is also the Social Progress Trust Fund established in fiscal 1961. It is available only to Latin American countries or investment in infrastructure, social overhead capital and housing. Since 1961, dollar-loans have been provided repayable in local currencies primarily through the Social Progress Trust Fund.

Food for Peace is an aid program that is the least costly to the United States and has been, up to now, also very "inexpensive" for the recipients. For they paid in their own currencies for the agricultural commodities.

Shipment of agricultural surplus commodities by the United States amounts to about 30 per cent of our official bilateral aid. These surpluses have accumulated in consequence of a domestic policy of price support and were not originally acquired by the United States Government in order to be distributed overseas. Congress, eager to develop constructive uses for the mounting agricultural surpluses, inserted in 1953 in the Mutual Security Act a provision (§ 550 of the MSA of 1951, as amended), requiring that, during fiscal year 1954, not less than $100 million of the funds appropriated for foreign aid be used to buy surplus agricultural products which could be sold abroad for foreign currencies. Though the Support Program of Farmer Prices is a burden to the American taxpayer, Food for Peace is not. Under Food for Peace agricultural commodities are sold for foreign currencies. The local currency may then be used for four major purposes:

(1) for United States uses in the recipient countries;
(2) for loans to private American and, in certain cases, foreign enterprises;
(3) for the recipient country, mainly as loans or grants for economic development and as grants for military purposes; and
(4) since fiscal 1967, for maternal welfare, child nutrition, and family planning.

With respect to loans to private American or foreign enterprises, local currencies up to 25 per cent of total sales may be loaned for business development and trade or to expand markets for, and consumption of, United States agricultural products. The provision, however, prohibits loans for the manufacture of products to be exported to the United States in competition with products produced in the United States, or for the manufacture or production of commodities to be marketed in competition with agricultural commodities or the products thereof.

With respect to loans or grants to the recipient country, it is obvious that if the United States gives back to the buyer the currency with which he bought the commodities, the United States has given him the commodities, whatever the legal hocus-pocus may be. Moreover, money itself is not a resource but a claim on a country's resources. Thus when the United States supplies a foreign country with the latter's own local currency, the United States is not increasing the real resources available to it but only giving it an additional claim on its own resources.

The Food for Peace program was reshaped for fiscal 1967. The main result of the change was a gradual shift from sales for local currency to dollar credit sales on relatively soft terms. This was designed to avoid the accumulation of foreign currencies and to alleviate the cost burden of the program.

Commodities under the Food for Peace program are generally priced at the prevailing United States export prices, whereas shipments under Title II of the Act — relating to emergency relief — are valued at the United States Commodity Credit Corporation's domestic support levels which are about 20 per cent higher than world market prices. The latter shipments therefore overstate the export market value of the commodities.

Generally it can be said that if our agricultural surplus commodities had been offered on the world market, the prices would have dropped and the aid given would have appeared considerably smaller.

By including expenditures that would almost certainly have been made by the United States Government for agricultural commodities and military equipment, even if there were no foreign aid program, the statistics probably had overstated by 1961 the aid burden by $10 to $20 billion.

If we look for total United States *aid commitments* by regions and programs for fiscal years 1946–1965, we find the following:

Regions	Total Aid		Economic					Military
	Bill of §	Per-cent	A. I. D.	SPTF (1)	PL 480 (2)	Exim (3)	Other	
Europe	46.7	100	32	. . .	5	7	21	35
Near East and South Asia ...	23.6	100	38	. . .	27	4	4	27
Africa	3.2	100	52	. . .	26	12	4	6
Far East	26.1	100	33	. . .	8	3	18	38
Latin America ..	10.4	100	29	5	13	35	10	8
Total	116.1	100	34	2	11	8	16	30

Header note: Fiscal Year 1946-1965

(1) Social Progress Trust Fund.
(2) Food for Peace.
(3) Export-Import Bank Loans (not including refundings).

In earlier years, the United States gave commodity and service *grants* as well as dollar *grants* which could be used by the recipient to acquire needed goods and services in the cheapest available markets. Dollar *grants,* however, have since 1959 no longer been authorized. This means that all new commitments are completely tied to United States procurement.

Grants versus loans has given rise to controversies abroad as well as at home. Russia's aid has been almost always in the form of loans. Rebellion against loans and insistence on grants was the basic issue in the Sino-Soviet split, beginning in 1957. The Chinese thought in the fifty's was the same as Europe's thought in the forty's—that the affluent society should help the destitute by grants, rather than loans. Russia refused; and the result was a vast withdrawal of Russian engineers and Russian-designed plans for factories and other industrial establishments.

Our AID assistance was placed increasingly on a loan basis until fiscal year 1966. In fiscal 1966, grants exceeded loans for the first time since fiscal 1961, due to a substantial increase in grants for Vietnam.

Outside AID, most of the economic bilateral aid is extended as loans. The Food for Peace program, however, has left the door open for grants, as far as the local currency proceeds from sales of agricultural commodities are given back to the buyer. But such grants are not additional aid, as they will not finance increased imports and therefore cannot substitute for dollar aid.

With reference to contributions to multilateral agencies, United States contributions to such agencies as the International Development Association have the effect of grants by the American taxpayer that are never repaid to the United States even though they become loans to the eventual recipient.

Though the United States shifted in the middle fifties from an emphasis on grants to an emphasis on loans, a large part of our loans have been very much grantlike. Many dollar loans have been repayable in foreign currencies. Between 1954 and 1961 the predecessor agencies of AID extended loans that could be repaid over a period of thirty or forty years at low interest rates and in foreign currency. Before 1957, practically all loans extended to less developed countries were repayable in foreign currency. But since 1961, all AID loans have been repayable only in dollars. Out of the $9.9 billion in loans which the AID and predecessor agencies committed through fiscal 1965, $2.4 billion are repayable in foreign currencies, of which $1.3 billion are in the currencies of Burma, Guinea, India, Israel, Pakistan, Poland, the U.A.R., and Yugoslavia. After 1961, dollar-loans repayable in foreign currencies have been provided through the Social Progress Trust Fund. This means that countries other than those of Latin America can no longer get dollar-loans repayable in foreign currencies.

Loans, even when repayable in dollars and tied to United States procurement, have a grant element if the interest rates which are charged are below the commercial ones, or if maturity periods are abnormaly long, or if a grace period for repaying the principal is accorded.

In 1964 the average interest rate increased from 2.5 per cent to 3.3 per cent; the average repayment period declined from thirty-three to twenty-eight years.

The increase of the average interest rate reflected an increase in the minimum AID interest rate from .75 per cent to 2 per cent in

January 1964 and to 2.5 per cent in October, 1964. Since for the first ten years most AID loans continue to carry only nominal interest rates, the effect of the higher minimum interest rate on actual interest payments will, therefore, not be felt until a considerable time to come.

Beyond this statutory minimum the actual terms of AID loans are established for each country on the basis of its overall foreign exchange position and development prospects — particularly, its probable future capacity to service foreign exchange debt. During fiscal 1965, seventy-nine of the eighty-six AID development loans carried the minimum interest rate and maturities of forty years. An AID study in 1965 forecast economic setbacks in the less developed countries unless the developed countries of the free world improved their lending terms.

AID loan terms are, however, hardened when a transitional country approaches self-supporting growth and an ability to finance further development from conventional international borrowing sources. During fiscal year 1965, seven loans in four countries were provided at harder terms — 3.5 per cent interest, twenty- to twenty-five year maturity, and three- to five-year grace periods. These loans at harder terms constituted 6 per cent of the total AID loan commitments for the period.

Export-Import bank loans are extended at relatively hard terms. They are repayable only in dollars at 5.75 per cent since the mid-1950's and 5.5 per cent since 1964 and most of these loans extend over a period of from five to twenty-five years.

The World Bank, which since February, 1966, has charged 6 per cent interest on loans to developing countries, raised its rate to 6.25 per cent at the start of 1968. Apart from the questions of loans versus grants and the terms of repayment for loans, "tied" aid presents an additional problem for developing countries receiving United States assistance. One cannot tell from the balance-of-payments statement what portion of United States aid has taken the form of exports of domestically produced commodities and services, but the information can be derived from other sources.

Military assistance consists principally of the provision of United States produced military equipment. Taking into account the cost of United States personnel overseas to administer the program, some oversea training costs, and other oversea expenditures, the estimates are that over 85 per cent of military assistance expenditures are made directly in the United States and the remainder are made offshore.

Aid committed by AID and predecessor agencies has become increasingly tied to United States procurement. During the Marshall Plan and most of the 1950's, aid appropriations were, in general, spent wherever in the world prices were lowest. During the Marshall Plan period most of the aid dollars, although not tied to United States procurement, were spent in this country. Beginning in 1959, in response to the changed situation of the United States balance of payments, the policy respecting aid purchases was changed. Today, with small exceptions, aid appropriations can only be spent in the United States for goods and services produced in this country. This change in appropriation policy, however, did not show in expenditure figures until 1961-1962. In 1961 commodity expenditures amounted to 44 per cent; they rose to 90 per cent in 1966, and for the first nine months of 1967 they rose to 96 per cent.

In 1965, 85 per cent of the new commitments (as opposed to expenditures) of AID were tied to United States procurement. It is estimated that the proportion spent in the United States for goods and services will be from 85 per cent to 90 per cent.

AID expenditures in calendar year 1964 were almost exactly $2 billion, of which $1.6 billion were directly spent in the United States. The dollar drain of AID-aid expenditures was accordingly $400 million. In 1964, $150 million were received in repayments, so the net cost was not $400 million, but $250 million. Not considering repayments, one can say that in calendar year 1964 for every dollar of AID aid extended, only 20 cents showed as a current adverse impact on our balance of payments. Put the other way around, 80 per cent of AID expenditures represented not dollars going abroad, but steel, machinery, fertilizers, and other goods and services purchased in the United States.

William S. Gaud, the Administrator of AID, testified in February 1968 before the House Foreign Affairs Committee that direct dollar outflows resulting from AID assistance programs totaled $290 million during fiscal 1967. He observed further that in fiscal 1969 it was expected that such outflows would total only 6 per cent of AID expenditures, or $130 million, and that about $220 million in anticipated principal and interest repayments would more than offset this outflow.

All loans of the Social Progress Trust Fund are tied to procurement in the member countries of the Inter-American Development Bank.

Food for Peace: Surplus agricultural commodities exported under Pub. L. 480 are, by definition, of domestic origin. Virtually all of the expenditures under this program are made directly in the United States, with only minor and unavoidable offshore costs in foreign ports.

The Export-Import Bank makes loans primarily to finance the export of United States goods.

As for the remaining assistance under the heading "Other U. S. Economic Programs" (including the capital subscription to international agencies and grants for the Peace Corps), it cannot be said how much has been spent in the United States. But it is estimated that a substantial share of the total expenditures of these international organizations are made in the United States.

For example, of the Peace Corps aid, 75 per cent is spent in the United States.

Although American foreign aid is by far the largest of any single country, the economic assistance furnished by those states that are members of the Organization for Economic Cooperation and Development (OECD) has been considerable. Currently, there are twenty-one member countries, including the United States, France, the United Kingdom, Germany, and Switzerland, while Yugoslavia and Finland possess a special status. The aid functions of the OECD are coordinated by a Development Assistance Committee (DAC), composed of the principal donors of aid among OECD countries plus Australia. This Committee, at the time of its annual Aid Review, subjects each country's aid program to detailed examination and discussion.

From 1961 to 1965, the total net flow of aid from these countries came to about $35 billion (including both bilateral aid and contributions to multilateral organizations, but excluding private investment and credits). This figure represents over 91 per cent of the total net flow from all industrial countries. Yet, during the 1961-1965 period, there was little expansion in the total net aid originating in OECD/DAC countries. The total annual flow of resources to underdeveloped countries from all sources rose from less than $8 billion in 1960 to about $11 billion in 1965, but these gains were the result of increased private investment and contributions from multilateral organizations.

Foreign aid is not confined to the Western world. Economic assistance from the Sino-Soviet bloc to developing countries dates back to 1954, when the Soviet Union set up a program. Her first substantial disbursements, however, were not made until 1956. Since then, other centrally planned economies have joined in providing economic assistance to less-developed countries.

Disbursements from Sino-Soviet countries provide the largest block of aid to underdeveloped countries outside of that from members of the OECD/DAC. But exact figures for actual disbursements are not readily available since Sino-Soviet aid is managed on a commitments basis and disbursements have fallen far behind commitments. Available statistics differ somewhat, but in general, it is believed that only between 30 per cent to 40 per cent of the total commitments between 1954 and 1965 were paid during that period. One estimate places total commitments by the end of 1965 at $7.8 billion; total disbursements would thus range between $2.3 billion and $3.1 billion.

The bulk of economic aid is extended in the form of loans, and is tied to the donor as well as to specified projects. About two-thirds of the total commitments of the Sino-Soviet bloc are attributed to the Soviet Union. The majority of loans by the Soviet Union carry an interest rate 2.5 per cent and are repayable over twelve years. Repayment begins one year after the delivery of the goods or completion of the project financed by the credit. Interest is charged only on the amount actually drawn. Repayments are usually made in the form of local products, but most credit arrangements provide for settlement in convertible currencies if no satisfactory form of repayment in kind can be found.

Loans extended by countries of eastern Europe carry somewhat higher interest rates, up to 5 per cent, and are repayable over a period of four to eight years.

Most loans from Peking are interest-free, repayable over a long period with an extended grace period. Some African countries and Ceylon have even received Chinese grants in pounds sterling and Swiss francs.

The composition of Sino-Soviet aid shows that more than one-half of it is used for manufacturing purposes, while about 35 per cent goes to multipurpose projects and agriculture, transport and communications, and mineral surveys and exploration.

The Sino-Soviet countries have made small contributions of less than $10 million a year to United Nations technical assistance and relief programs. Compared with those of the Western industrialized countries, contributions to multilateral agencies are fairly negligible. Except for Yugoslavia, the Sino-Soviet bloc does not contribute to the International Bank for Reconstruction and Development (IBRD) and its affiliates, the International Development Association and the International Finance Corporation; nor, except for Yugoslavia, are Sino-Soviet countries members of the International Monetary Fund. They do, however, contribute to the funds of various UN agencies such as EPTA (the Expanded Program of Technical Assistance), UNICEF (the United Nations Children's Fund), and UNSF (the United Nations Special Fund).

Sino-Soviet aid has fanned to all continents — altogether to thirty-eight countries (including Bolivia, Cuba, Cyprus, Iceland, Laos, Turkey, and Yugoslavia) — as compared to around 100 countries helped by the United States since 1945. Aid has been greatest in the countries of Africa and the Far East. In particular, aid to Afghanistan, India, Indonesia and the U.A.R. amounted to over half of the total cumulative commitments through 1964.

Military aid is the saddest chapter of our foreign aid adventure. Over three-fourths of our military aid for 1968 has been allotted to five nations adjacent to the Soviet Union or the Peking regime, namely, Greece, Turkey, Iran, Formosa, and Korea. Most of these are totalitarian regimes that have no political formula for turning back any tide of communism. They are countries that could easily be destroyed or captured if World War III broke out. About one-fifth of our military aid for 1968 is to developing countries that have no Communist neighbors. This military aid can only serve one function and that is to put in the hands of the powers-that-be the ability to suppress any dissident elements in their own population.

A partial antedote to United States military aid is the Act on November 14, 1967, which authorizes the President to measure the amount of foreign aid in light of the percentage of the recipient's budget that is devoted to military purposes and the degree to which the recipient is using its foreign exchange to acquire military equipment. And he is authorized to terminate the aid if he finds that the aid is being diverted to military ends or the recipient is using its own resources for unnecessary military expenditures.

A developing nation that acquires an expensive military superstructure is apt to forget or postpone the basic educational, agricultural, medical, social, and industrial wants that plague it.

We started our military aid with a grant program and then by a series of steps began to sell it, making credit financing available. This military sales program grew considerably, amounting to $11.1 billion between 1962 and 1966. About 11 per cent of these sales went to the developing world, about 8 per cent going to the Near East and South Asia. The credit sales during 1968 carry a 5.5 per cent interest rate with a seven-year repayment period. The overall military aid from both the Western countries and the Sino-Soviet group is difficult to estimate. So far as developing countries are concerned, they probably expended from 1963 to 1964 about $8 billion on defense.

We, along with Soviet Russia and the Peking regime, have probably done more to promote military dictatorships than any power in modern times. Our policy partly originated in the need of the Pentagon to dispose of its "used car" equipment. Obsolescence produces vast quantities of tanks, planes, machine guns, artillery, and the like, and we have armed the dictatorships of the world with them. The bald truth is that sales of military equipment are produced for the Cold War in which ideological allies are sought. But the ally with whom we end up is usually a dictator who uses his newly acquired weapons to strengthen his hold on his nation, to police his restless subjects, and to put down reformers.

In an earlier lecture I mentioned the two Maryknoll fathers in Guatemala who joined the cause of the peasants against the oligarchy composed of the landlords and the army. The role which United States military aid played in the Guatemala situation is summarized by them as follows:

> The U. S. government has sent jets, helicopters, weapons, money and military advisers to the government that only strengthens its control over the peasant masses. This past year, 1967, salaries, uniforms, arms and vehicles for 2,000 new policemen were paid for by the Alliance for Progress. This year another 1,500 are projects for enlistment, to say nothing about the secret intelligence services rendered for ferreting out all "social disturbers."
>
> The U. S. Church also contributes to this aggravating situation: building fine rectories, convents, schools and churches throughout Latin America, distributing all kinds of food, medicine, and clothing that only succeed in temporarily quieting the restlessness of the less foresighted. U. S. churchmen strengthen the already decaying hierarchical structure by building seminaries (that will soon be empty), by aiding the Latin bishops to organize themselves on diocesan and national levels, which only tighten their social and economic control over the people.
>
> For the money and the personnel that they receive from the U. S.,

many in Latin America are willing to sacrifice all vestiges of the national identity of their flocks in order to make them little U. S. ghettos.

It was American weapons that put down the seething popular discontent in Iran. I remember a message I received from the CIA ten years ago concerning Iran. I had been associated with Nationalists who had tried hard to introduce political and economic justice to that benighted kingdom. Symbolic of that movement was the late Mohammed Mossadegh whom we helped depose. After he ended in prison, American military aid mounted. The whispered CIA message I received at a Washington, D.C., reception in the late 1950's was this: "Now Iran is so heavily armed that the people will never be able to rise again."

That prophecy turned out to be true.

Those who fill the jails of Iran are impotent against these American weapons. The clubs used in Iran to crack the skulls of dissidents are deeply engraved with the symbol "Made in the USA." While the CIA spent millions to overthrow Mossadegh, the "consideration" which the United States received was a 40 per cent interest in the oil consortium that Iran now finds onerous.

We are not the only transgressors. Russia too is very active in arming its bloc of nations. The progress toward arming the developing nations indeed brings the Great Powers closer and closer to the brink of nuclear disaster, for the presence of these tremendously destructive weapons in the hands of feudal reactionaries makes it possible for any country, no matter how small and underdeveloped, to perpetuate its feud with neighbors even as respects outworn controversies. Though Israel is a legal, living, vibrant entity, Nasser buys military equipment to destroy her, even though it means mortgaging Egypt for the indefinite future.

The aid extended by the industrialized nations to the developing countries has not exceeded 0.7 per cent of the GNP of the developed nations, if the annual total inflow of capital, both public and private, is computed. The rate of contribution has been falling as appropriations get caught up in domestic politics and the rich get tired of extending aid.

Many developing nations already have their future heavily mortgaged for principal and interest payments. Military aid alone has Egypt mortgaged to the hilt; and India with its vast development plans has already pledged her future to debt service.

Some experts think that we may soon see in some areas a point of equilibrium where inflow of capital almost balances service on the old debt. All of which has led David Horowitz of Israel to say, "The institutions engaged in promoting economic development may reach a peak of respectability but it will also be a peak of futility."

A development program when viewed from the interior of a developing nation is often filled with despair. The water reservoir, the DDT plant, the textile mill is in evidence. But making the interest payments and amortization leaves precious little for further development.

The total collections for interest and principal (of AID and predecessor agencies) amounted to $2,176 million through June 30, 1965. Following is a table showing the collections, broken down as between dollar collections and local currency collections.

[Millions of dollars]

	Dollar receipts	Dollar Equivalent of local currency receipts	Total
Interest collections	$591.2	$522.6	$1,113.8
Principal repayments	801.6	260.7	1,062.3
Total......................	1,392.8	783.3	2,176.1

Between 1946 and 1965, countries in the Near East and South Asia, the Far East, Latin America, and Africa paid to the United States about $5 billion in principal and interest. And this figure promises to increase rapidly due to the impact of our current preference for loans.

Thus, the developing countries are not getting their aid free; nor are we losing many dollars as a result of our aid programs.

One of the most comprehensive proposals for assisting developing countries emerged from the October, 1967, ministerial meeting of a group of developing countries, known as the Group of 77. The proposal, entitled the Charter of Algiers, is a sign that the less developed countries are turning more and more to the UN for a solution to their many problems. The Charter begins with an appraisal of the current development problems facing the less developed countries — among them being a slow average per annum increase in per capita income, a decline in the share of total world exports, loss of purchasing power, increasing indebtedness, the lack of capital and skilled labor to implement modern technology, an increase in the degree of trade protection in the developed countries, implicit discrimination in tariff policies toward less developed countries, the decrease in aid from developed countries as a percentage of their gross national product, and the general hardening of the terms and conditions of development finance.

To remedy these ills, the Charter suggests various steps that should be taken:

(1) the conclusion of international commodity agreements, in cocoa and sugar immediately, and in other commodities—such as bananas, rubber, tea, iron ore, tobacco, and cotton—as soon as possible;

(2) the provision of additional financial and technical assistance by developed countries and international financial institutions to facilitate diversification programs in commodities;

(3) liberalization of trade by taking such steps as: the removal of all restrictions and charges applied to primary products (including processed and semi-processed products) originating exclusively in less developed countries; the elimination of tariff and non-tariff barriers; allocation by developed countries of a minimum share of their domestic markets to competing products from developing countries; the beginning of studies and assistance to improve the competitive position of products of developing countries affected by synthetics and substitutes from developed countries; the establishment of a general system of tariff preferences on a non-discriminatory and non-reciprocal basis for all manufactures and semi-manufactures from less developed countries (including all processed and semi-processed primary products); and the establishment of objective criteria for application of trade restrictions implemented by developed countries under escape clauses such as "market disruption" or "special circumstances";

(4) the elimination of preferences to some developing countries—for which other steps would have to be taken to ensure that those

countries losing present preferences would continue to receive advantages equal to what they would lose by abolition;

(5) the promotion of trade in developing countries by such means as diversification of production, technical and financial assistance, and the dissemination of trade information;

(6) improvement in the flow of capital to less developed countries for development financing by agreements by developed countries to advance a minimum of 1% of their GNP in net aid on the basis of actual disbursements; the intensification of support to regional development banks; and the establishment of the International Bank for Reconstruction and Development as a financial institution exclusively for less developed countries;

(7) the softening of terms and conditions for development finance; alleviation of the debt-servicing burdens of the less developed countries by consolidation of their external debts into long-term obligations with low interest rates: measures that do not bear the name David Horowitz but which are almost verbatim the same ones that he has proposed, as I will shortly relate;

(8) reduction of the cost of certain invisibles, such as freight rates and reinsurance;

(9) encouraging the transfer of technology and knowledge to developing countries by allowing industrial patents to be used on lenient terms;

(10) encouraging joint efforts among less developed countries through trade expansion and economic integration;

(11) taking special measures in favor of the least developed among the developing nations, including special consideration in relaxing trade barriers and temporary refunds of revenue charges and duties on commodities of particular interest to the least developed countries.

The Charter of Algiers is significant because it represents coordinated action among the less developed countries in taking the initiative. But, as the proposals themselves indicate, such action will be fruitless without cooperation from the developed countries in matters of trade and aid.

If both aid and trade are to become real forces in raising the standards of developing countries, a new federalism — certainly in spirit and hopefully in form — will be needed.

Village Renovation

Village development programs — designed essentially to build roads, construct bridges, locate and seal springs, erect dams, build schools and community centers — have been financed by AID. Beyond this is the need to tackle the festering problem of the villages of the world. These villages are worse places for humans than our barns and pens are for cattle and hogs. They have none of the amenities of civilization — no drugs, not even aspirin; no sidewalks; often, no toilets; no schools; no first-aid, let alone medical and dental care. They are miserable sites that often can be smelled at a long distance.

The inhabitants are illiterate and filled with despair, discontent, and disease. The erection of the finest factories in the world will leave them untouched. Yet they contain and condition the most valuable resources of any country — the people.

If we are to have viable societies, as well as modern ones, these villages must be renovated and become healthy, happy centers where people are enlightened as well as fed and clothed.

The ultimate thrust of the world's present problem reaches renovation of the villages where the bulk of the people live, where illiteracy is the norm, and where habit and superstition take the place of scientific knowledge. The village is, I think, the starting point for the solution of all the problems of the developing nations. It will implicate many international agencies.

The first effort to renovate the village was started in the 1930's on the mainland of China by a group headed by James Yen. It never received the blessing of the corrupt and reactionary regime of Chiang Kai Shek but nonetheless it established important pilot projects. In the China Act of 1948, we made provision for financing a Joint Commission on Rural Reconstruction for the renovation of China's villages. This was an international agency, two members being American and three Chinese. It operated in China until driven out by the Communists and then moved to Taiwan. The burgeoning agricultural economy of Taiwan is due largely to the work of that international agency.

James Yen, who was a member of JCRR, formed a private group

which launched this rural reconstruction program in other nations, always working with and through a local indigenous group. That program is now in full force in the Philippines, Colombia, and Guatemala; and plans are afoot to launch it also in Thailand and in South Korea.

Like the one launched in Taiwan, it has a fourfold program:

Health. Water supplies are protected against pollution. Sanitary outhouses are built. Screening against flies, pasteurization of milk, boiling of water and the like are taught. Vaccinations are given. A first-aid station is established.

Education. Schools are built, teachers hired, books and libraries are supplied. Adult literacy courses are installed.

Agricultural and other Livelihood. Modern methods of seed selection, tilling, planting, and spraying are introduced. Cross-breeding is used for improved productivity of chickens, pigs, and other livestock. Fertilizers are introduced. Credit unions and other cooperatives are formed. Handicrafts and cottage industries are introduced.

Self-government. The villagers are trained and organized for managing the affairs of the village, through village councils and other like groups. They do the planning and policing and provide the general supervision of all local affairs.

A similar program has been in effect in other countries, notably India, where about 600,000 villages have been renovated at least to a degree.

But there probably has never been such a sparkling renovation as that experienced in the Philippines.

Dr. Yen's group soon learned that agricultural technology cannot be exported, because what worked in the temperate zone often failed in a different climate. And so it was that his group established the Institute for Rural Reconstruction in the Philippines, of which I am the chairman, where adaptive research is undertaken and where village trainees from like zones are brought for intensive education.

Between May, 1953, and December, 1967, the Philippine Rural Reconstruction Movement (PRRM) had extended its fourfold program (health, education, livelihood, and self-government) into 413 villages, or barrios, of which 126 are still being assisted. This number represents only a small fraction (1.4 per cent) of the total number of barrios (almost 30,000) in the Philippines. But those barrios which have been reached by PRRM are pilot projects whose results are reflected in other barrios. The success of the program caused the

Philippine Government to establish a special agency for a national Community Development Program.

The implementation of the program is done by workers who live in the barrios full time for at least two years. They are university or college-trained graduates. Before they are assigned to the barrios, they undergo training for six months. From 1954 to 1967 PRRM trained a total of 411 university or college graduates for rural reconstruction work. About 200 of those are still working in the program. The others have transferred to other agencies, governmental or private, also doing rural development work, thus spreading with them the influence of the Movement.

Its influence is also spread through the training of workers for community development in foreign countries. The largest groups from private organizations which have come to the Philippines for training at the Institute are those from Guatemala and Colombia. Sixteen participants from each of those countries went through training for four months, and then returned to their respective countries to start the implementation of privately supported community development programs, one in each country. In addition, a total of 125 Peace Corps Volunteers have gone through training in community development at the Institute. Other trainees have undergone training there from a few days to a few weeks.

As to health, infant mortality has dropped from 101.06 per thousand to 68.05 per thousand; maternal mortality from 3.7 per thousand to 2.0 per thousand.

As to livelihood, the records of production of over two thousand demonstration farmers in 106 of the barrios show a substantial increase in production and income. The average annual income per farmer in the region from which the demonstration farmers were selected is about 700 pesos, which is largely from a single crop (rice). (The average yearly income per farmer for the Philippines as a whole is only 500 pesos.) The PRRM program taught farmers to diversify their production and thereby increase their income. The demonstration farmers were shown how to improve their methods of rice culture, engage in hoe gardening, improve the breeds of their native chickens, up-grade their native swine, and produce secondary crops, such as onions and vegetables, on a semi-commercial scale. The farmers were urged to undertake these activities during the off-season for their major crop, when they would otherwise have been idle most of the time.

Many other farmers have followed the practices of the demonstration farmers in selecting better seeds, planting secondary crops, and improving the breeds of their chickens and swine. As a result, the farmers in the villages assisted by PRRM have increased their income considerably, perhaps by 30 per cent or more. The average income of the demonstration farmer increased 126.5 per cent for the five years 1961–1966.

The literacy and self-government programs have had an electrifying grassroots effect. Historically, the governor of the province appointed the village government. Now the villages elect their own. Originally all taxes collected in the village were sent to the province for expenditure. As a result of the growing political consciousness of the villagers, a change has been made; now 10 per cent of the local revenues are left to the local unit for administration. Those two changes required national legislation.

So far, there has been no attempt among the farmers to pool their parcels of land to enable them to use machinery profitably. Farmers in three villages, however, long ago contemplated pooling their credits to buy electric pumps to irrigate their farms and small tractors to plow their fields. The first known attempt by the farmers to use cooperatives for marketing their farm products in villages assisted by the PRRM occurred in 1967 at a meeting held between 17 village leaders. The leaders from eight villages agreed to plant peanuts on a minimum of 50 hectares for each village (125 acres each), the products to be sold under a cooperative marketing agreement.

The PRRM is now embarking on a new project called Multi-Service (Farmers) Reconstruction Associations (MRA). These associations will be designed to unify the administration of already existing credit and consumers' cooperatives and marketing and machinery cooperatives yet to be created.

All but one of the cooperatives presently assisted by PRRM are credit cooperatives, financed principally from the fixed deposits of the members. There are ninety-five of these cooperatives with a total membership of 6,650.

Philippine bank loans are particularly burdensome when it comes to the consumers. Real estate security is usually demanded as collateral. Terms of repayment demanded by the banks are usually on a monthly basis, and additional charges such as notarial fees and inspection fees are very onerous. One learns in Asia that the banks, as well as the countries, are underdeveloped.

United Nations agencies — notably UNESCO and FAO — have been working on segments of these village problems around the world.

The Community Development Program, launched in India in 1952, has now reached all of the 600,000 villages. Its work laid the basis for the present agricultural revolution in India — a revolution in farming techniques that nearly 20 per cent of the village areas of India have already experienced.

Latin America fairly cries out for some such program. Yet the Alliance for Progress turned its back on village programs and would have nothing to do with them. It has, through its enormous financial resources, been nudging a few countries into land reform. But land reform without village renovation can be a sad spectacle. Come with me to Latin America, and I will show you where land reform, which we have helped finance, has ended with the members of the Establishment getting the choice bottom lands and the *campesino* the hilly, inferior top lands. A *campesino* turned loose for the first time on his own is bewildered in his ignorance, and does not know even when to plant and when to harvest. There have been, as a result, great tragedies. Thus, where sisal is the main crop, the newly liberated villagers are bankrupt when the world price falls. There are no agriculture agents on hand to teach them how to raise substitute crops or how to become diversified farmers. After land distribution, as well as before, the members of the Establishment flourish, but the *campesino* lives on or below the edge of subsistence. The reason is the prejudice of the Alliance for Progress in favor of the Establishment, and its lack of interest in and true knowledge of the countryside where the *campesino* lives. The Alliance for Progress prefers to deal with the elite, not with the revolutionaries. For this we face an awful accounting.

Conclusion

Population. Runaway population growth is as enervating to the societies of underdeveloped nations as drops in prices of their exports or increases in prices of their imports. Populations are multiplying 3 per cent annually, doubling within a generation, and multiplying eighteen-fold in a century. The situation is so serious that according to the experts the *Time of Famines* will begin by 1975 and be on full display by 1984. A concentrated attack on problems holding back agricultural production is one front. The other is all-out population control efforts. Unless our numbers and our food production are matched, the world faces not only hunger, poverty, and disease, but bitterness and violence that will overflow all frontiers.

Americans who have not traveled abroad have no idea of the impact of mounting population in a developing country. We feel that impact here in terms of crowded urban conditions, disappearing wilderness areas, decreasing open spaces, highway congestion, smog, and so on. But one has to travel abroad to see with his own eyes what the burgeoning population can do to already poverty-stricken areas. Perhaps the most picturesque, moving account was written by James P. Brown of *The Times*:

> If you took all of America's thirty million poor, crammed them into a state the size of South Carolina, cut the average income to a figure less than 10 per cent of the amount received by a family on welfare in New York City and reduced food rations to a daily handful of rice, you would have a situation somewhat approaching that in the Indian state of West Bengal.
>
> Take 10 per cent of these indigent millions, including a high proportion of men separated from their families, and jam them into a city the size of Chicago but with the facilities of an American frontier town of a century ago, you have a rough approximation of Calcutta, West Bengal's capital and India's largest city.

Population control accordingly comes first when the problems of the developing nations are faced. Mounting population has already offset *per capita gains* in GNP in some nations. Mounting population has indeed reduced a net gain to zero or less. Education in birth control comes then as the prime aid of the modern nations to the developing ones.

Military expenditures to put the new ruling group in total command over the people of a developing nation have also been depleting. Graft and corruption, which are more common than not, have a like effect. This trinity — military spending, corruption, population — has meant that in most developing nations the standard of living has been dropping even though aid has been increasing.

Trade. The industrialized nations with their resources and sophistication can be expected to take care of themselves when it comes to trade.

Agencies of the United Nations have set as the objective an attainment of a minimum annual growth rate of 5 per cent in the income of developing countries by 1970. That goal implies a certain level of imports, mainly of capital goods. An import growth rate of 6.5 per cent is considered to be necessary. But the merchandising has not grown at the desired rate, due largely to increased transport costs and interest payments on loans.

The developing countries need special dispensations that only some form of federalism can give.

The "richer" countries of Europe under the Marshall Plan were given grants to overcome the economic disaster of war. But our aid which is really intended to promote economic development of the "poor" or underdeveloped countries is mainly extended in the form of loans.

The Marshall Plan was designed to operate upon European initiative. It provided for a system of bilateral agreements between the various European countries and this country, by which the individual European states would commit themselves to increasing their production, attaining financial stability and reducing trade barriers. There was also the "counterpart" system, under which each government receiving aid would have to deposit funds in local currency equal to the amounts received in grants; those local funds were to be used in various ways to promote recovery. It was the responsibility of the European countries to work out their own recovery plans, which were then submitted to the United States for approval; administration of the Plan was entrusted to the Economic Cooperation Administration, a special agency established under the Marshall Plan legislation. Under the Plan, we invested about $13 billion in Europe, 86 per cent of that aid being in the form of grants.

The Marshall Plan system was molded to fit the nature and needs of Europe. We invested our money to aid Europe's recovery, not her development from a primitive state. From a political point of view, a strong Europe would counteract a strong Russia and her allies. From an economic point of view, Europe already possessed the skilled manpower, managerial skills, and experience needed to run an industrial complex efficiently. And she had the know-how to exercise competently the initiative given her under the Marshall Plan. Certainly the developing nations do not have the industrial base possessed by postwar Europe. The underdeveloped countries, moreover, generally have not shown the cooperative spirit that existed in postwar Europe, although the recent Group of 77 meeting perhaps signifies a change.

One of the best-known plans for helping the developing countries to increase their export earnings, and therefore increase their foreign exchange, is that of Raul Prebisch, the Secretary General of the United Nations Conference on World Trade and Development (UNCTAD). Prebisch noted that the developing countries would have to dispose of more foreign exchange if they were to progress at a satisfactory rate of growth. Neither free trade nor domestic industrialization was an adequate remedy; in the former case, imports by developed countries of primary commodities would grow too slowly as income increased, and in the latter, domestic markets would be too small. Although removal of agricultural barriers in the developed countries would be desirable, it would not present a satisfactory solution, because world demand for those commodities is increasing too slowly. Prebisch thus offered four specific suggestions for dealing with this "trade gap":

—giving temporary tariff preferences in the markets of developed countries to manufactured products from developing countries, thus helping the latter to expand their markets and compensate for initial costs of production;

—setting up customs unions and free trade areas among underdeveloped countries, again expanding the market and making possible greater specialization;

—establishing commodity markets to ensure higher prices for stable exports of the developing countries;

—providing a fund to compensate the developing countries in the case of long-term declining levels in export earnings, when those earnings fall below some predetermined level.

To expand a bit on these suggestions, it should be noted that only in the case of commodities produced mainly in developing countries and not subject to serious competition from substitutes (for example, coffee, tea, bananas, or tin) would a price-raising commodity agreement be likely to succeed. With respect to finance, special drawing rights have already been made available at the International Monetary Fund to bail out developing countries from an unexpected slump in their export receipts. Colombia turned to this to offset the sudden drop in her coffee export earnings. This compensatory scheme, however, should be broadened into a more general system which will cope with long-term shortfalls as well.

In the long run, the question of market access will determine the pace of economic development for the less developed nations. In this area, tremendous pressure from a new constellation of world politics and a new solidarity would be necessary to help less-developed countries at the expense of domestic interests in the developed countries. A major breakthrough would be the granting of tariff preferences to developing countries. Only preferential treatment will enable those countries to sell their products on the large markets of the industrialized states in order to earn the urgently needed foreign exchange for financing imports and promoting economic development. And to build up a consistent system of protectionism, the less developed countries would like to erect trade barriers against imports of the industrialized nations; such barriers would protect infant industries, and would divert imports from luxury and nonessential goods to those required at each country's individual stage of development. Under the current system, however, new or higher tariffs on imports in developing countries would have to be accepted by GATT. And although these protective tariffs would only have effects on the composition and not on the value of imports — since the developing countries need all their export proceeds to develop their economies — it would require a great deal of pressure to gain approval of any new barriers.

This idea of temporary tariff preferences to developing countries has United States support.

President Johnson said at Punta del Este in 1967:

> We are ready to explore with other industrialized countries — and with our own people — the possibility of temporary preferential tariff advantages for all developing countries in the markets of all the industrialized countries.

But that idea is at war with the philosophy and practice of the EEC which demands reciprocal treatment for its members whenever an outside or associated nation receives preferential treatment. And so the fate of developing nations will turn on whether the favorable American approach is taken or the more restrictive oppressive philosophy of EEC. The OECD ministerial meeting in Paris on November 30, 1967, did not forsake the EEC principle. It did, however, keep the door open a crack by establishing guidelines for discussion at the 1968 UNCTAD Conference which suggest temporary preferential tariff treatment by developed countries for manufactured and semi-manufactured goods from developing countries.

On a regional level, the member states of the OAS signed a protocol of amendment to the Charter in February, 1967, which in Article 37 encourages individual and collective measures to bring about the reduction or elimination of trade barriers that affect the exports of member states, except when those barriers are designed to speed up development or are related to national security or the need for economic balance. Improving conditions for trade in basic commodities through international agreements and adopting measures to promote market expansion are countenanced. International financial cooperation and diversification of exports are still other means mentioned to aid development. Finally, the member states provide in Article 38 of the protocol that they:

> . . . reaffirm the principle that when the more-developed countries grant concessions in international trade agreements that lower or eliminate tariffs or other barriers to foreign trade so that they benefit the less-developed countries, they should not expect reciprocal concessions from those countries that are incompatible with their economic development, financial, and trade needs.

This protocol, known as the Protocol of Buenos Aires, has been submitted by President Johnson to the Senate. But to date no action has been taken. Will this measure languish in the Senate for years before a two-thirds vote can be procured?

As this is being written, the 1968 UNCTAD Conference in New Delhi has just ended. The affluent nations, including of course the United States and Russia, were more concerned with their own economic and financial problems than with those of the developing nations. No preferential tariff treatment could be agreed upon. Even the developing nations were divided. The result was only "unanimous agreement in favor of the early establishment of a mutually acceptable system of generalized, nonreciprocal and nondiscriminatory preferences" — an agreement that obviously means nothing.

Aid. So far as aid is concerned, the developing nations have been receiving for investment about $20 billion a year; yet only $4 billion represent net capital transfers from the industrialized nations, the difference being service on the debt. There are ideal alternatives to the present system. It would be ideal if all industrialized nations, including of course Soviet Russia, would pool a certain percentage of their GNP and let that aid be disbursed by an international agency. Will a nation surrender the "political" power in the present aid system? The ability to "buy" a government or sway or influence it through a loan or grant is attractive. Will nations give it up?

The substitution of "grants" for "loans" is another ideal solution. But it too is not practical in the present frame of reference. As already noted, that was the critical demand that Peking made of Moscow in 1957 — the demand that led to a worsening of Sino-Soviet relations. It is the incessant demand that one hears on all the underdeveloped continents. It is the policy we pursued in the Marshall Plan and forsook under Eisenhower.

We touch now the very core of the international aid problems. It is around them that summit meeting after summit meeting must be held to try to find the formula whereby the industrialized nations as a unit can establish a viable relationship with the developing nations so that they can in time become regional entities that have somewhat the same relationship to the center as Appalachia and Harlem have to Washington, D.C.

The problem cannot even be rationally approached in the atmosphere of the Cold War. It is desperately complicated even when DeGaulle's France and Wilson's England are involved. But it is a central problem of the new world order that must be faced if the developing nations are not to plague the world with violence and disorder.

The idea of grants, of course, gets caught up in the domestic politics of the grantor. Grants to socialist-oriented nations are not feasible in American terms of reference as of the 50's and 60's. India still suffers from that label even though only 20 per cent of India's GNP is derived from the public sector as compared with 25 per cent in the United States. The international financial institutions to which the United States contributes heavily are also largely disabled from making grants.

Foreign aid even on a "loan" basis has difficult sledding at home. Many have felt that the use of foreign aid meant "buying up" a foreign nation in the Cold War context. So when an aid recipient voted against our position in the United Nations, it was not uncommon to have it proposed that all "aid" to that country be discontinued.

Foreign aid has been "sold" our people not so much on the basis of the need to build a viable world society as to further our own selfish interests. We have been conditioned to think of foreign aid in terms of benefits to ourselves. "Dollars sent abroad must be spent here" has been a powerful slogan.

Yet in spite of these narrow and prejudiced viewpoints, American contributions have continued throughout all periods, irrespective of national mood or national politics.

The Administration's foreign aid bill for fiscal 1968 was cut drastically by Congress to $2.3 billion, the lowest foreign aid appropriation in twenty years. For fiscal 1969, the president has requested slightly under $2.5 billion in economic aid. This was $132 million less than his request for fiscal 1968. In addition, he has requested $420 million for grant military aid, and $595 million for Supporting Assistance which, as already noted, is closely connected with military assistance. Judging from Congress' reaction during the foreign aid hearings of March, 1968, held amidst charges of mismanagement of funds by AID officials, the prospects are good for a cut in even this meagre economic assistance program for 1969. Yet when all is said and done, we have the best record in the field of all industrialized nations, even though our annual aid is less than three quarters of 1 per cent of our GNP.

The UN's Development Decade goal has been 1 per cent of the developed countries' resources in aid to developing countries. Many developed countries have contended, however, that "net" rather than "gross" resources are the appropriate measuring stick. The 1968 UNCTAD Conference, however, managed to agree upon a figure of 1 per cent of the developed countries' GNP. Yet, there was no agreement reached on a target date for implementation of that 1 per cent guideline. Apart from the percentage amount of GNP to be given in aid, we, and the other industrialized nations as well, need make some basic revisions in our system of aid. The carrying charges are too high for the developing nations. One modification is often stated in terms of "soft" rather than "hard" loans. The World Bank makes only "hard" loans as its funds are raised on commercial terms. The International Development Association, a member of the World Bank Group, makes "soft" loans; but the means at its disposal are quite limited. Yet if there is to be rapid progress on the industrial front, a radical innovation must be made. Interest must be drastically reduced, even to nominal amounts. This in effect would return us to the philosophy of the Marshall Plan by making a grant of the difference between nominal interest and the commercial rate.

David Horowitz of Israel is the chief proponent of this idea. He calls it "an interest equalization fund." It is to be accompanied by the opening up to developing nations of the financial markets of the industrialized nations where over $30 billion of fixed interest debentures and bonds are issued annually. Developing nations would seek these capital funds and the private loans would be guaranteed by the respective developed nation. Interest paid by the borrower would be nominal. The difference between it and the interests on the bond would be paid from an "equalization fund" supplied by the respective developed nations. David Horowitz thinks that this system of nominal interest and government guaranteed loans could easily result in an allocation of 1.5 per cent of the GNP of industrialized nations to the developing ones, which would more than double the present rate. This rate, plus 15 per cent savings by the developing nations, would, in his view, make impressive improvements in the conditions of the developing nations within the next decade.

American financiers look askance at this proposal, saying it is impractical. We face here, as in 1929, the need to reexamine, renovate, and readjust conventional banking attitudes and approaches. We need an inventive genius to design new approaches and new solutions. If, to use the words of David Horowitz, the world becomes a "prisoner of its own prejudices" there will be a collision course between rich and poor at the planetary level.

When it comes to military aid to developing nations, Russia is probably the prime offender. But we certainly come second. Why developing nations in Latin America, Africa, the Middle East, and Asia need jet fighter planes and tanks is hard to imagine. There are exceptions. Israel, invaded at least seventy-five times in 1966, faces the prospect of annihilation. India, actually invaded in mass by Peking, is forced to use resources needed for development for defense. But most neighbors are friendlier and the dangers of wars of extermination among them are quite theoretical. An insistence of the Great Powers on a Rule of Law for resolving territorial disputes and disputes over waterways will reduce those conflicts practically to zero.

A nation rich in oil may not get bogged down with debt service on armament sales. But most developing nations cannot afford the luxury. Many already have their future earnings pledged for these needless commodities. And as aid becomes more clearly a function of the international community, a consensus must be sought between the Great Powers to put an end to this armament program. It probably can never be done under the regime of the Cold War. But the Cold War is an anachronism in this age where the stake of all humanity is in the prevention of war. Riddance of the Cold War can be realized only if the international community is sufficiently cooperative to help design and build an international welfare state.

A rich "socialist" nation can be as exploitive of a developing nation as a rich "capitalist" nation. The basic economic facts are the same, no matter which label is given the rich: the primary products which the developing nation must sell are cheap; the industrial articles it needs are expensive. Che Guevara made the point in 1965:

> We should not speak any more about developing mutually beneficial trade based on prices which are really disadvantageous to the under-developed countries because of the law of value and the unequal relations of international trade caused by that law. How can "mutual benefit" mean the selling at world market prices of raw materials that cost the underdeveloped countries unlimited sweat and suffering and the buying at world market prices of machines produced in large, modern, mechanized factories?

The fear that the poor have of the rich cuts across all ideological lines. As the tension between East and West has somewhat lessened, the fear is that the North (both capitalist and Communist) will be pitted against the South (the developing nations).

We have witnessed in the past a world-market system designed to transfer wealth from the poor to the rich. We must now design the opposite regime.

Village Reform. The new welfare state for any developing nation starts with the renovation of the villages, a program that must extend beyond sanitary and educational measures. It must promote political activities such as the formation of cooperatives and land reform. It must seek to provide political equality, equal justice under law, and the peaceful cooperation of all classes in designing a new society.

There is no other way than education and enlightenment to provide economic and political democracy. There is no other way to protect existing agricultural serfs against some oligarchy — political, financial, religious, or familial.

Technical assistance must come from overseas, whether it be an Israeli team (ORT) teaching telecommunications in Guinea, a Japanese team changing rice culture in India, or an Iowa farmer showing

Latinos how to revolutionize corn production. These ideas must come from overseas because that is the source of the agricultural as well as industrial technological revolutions.

But the overseas contribution must reach to the vitals and help the local people renovate all the villages. Otherwise the future is bleak, for it has the prospect of developing dozens upon dozens of Vietnams.

American foreign aid has studiously avoided village reform programs to promote rural reconstruction. Dr. Yen pounded long and hard on the door of the Alliance For Progress. But no one would listen. For the Alliance For Progress is little more than a tool of the Establishment ensconced in Latin America. There is no ideological or political reason why our hands should be tied or why we should hesitate. The success of our Marshall Plan, however, set us on another path and the Washington, D. C., bureaucracy became conditioned and controlled by that concept. The theory is that if we create in these benighted lands a new middle class, we will have the best possible rampart against communism. But as the years pass, the rich get richer and the poor get poorer. We now face an overwhelming world crisis at the village level. Help must come from the outside. Private groups such as James Yen's can be the pacesetters. But existing international agencies must be encouraged (or new ones created) not to reconstruct the villages of the world but to inspire local groups to launch such programs and then with lavish technical and financial assistance to push hard for complete renovation of these rural ghettos which are now points of a dangerous infection.

We face today an emerging international democracy that needs the healing influence of the welfare state if it is not to be torn apart by dissensions and wrecked by attitudes of despair and futility.

Various types and degrees of federalism are indeed necessary for immediate adoption unless the rich get so rich and the poor get so poor as to cause the world to fragmentize dangerously.

Chapter IV

The Brain Drain
and the Developing Nations

The arrival of industrialization is not always a cure all. New perplexing political problems are often presented. One will find even in India tremendous pressure upon a new plant to take on more workers than it needs for efficient operation. In any country where unemployment is high, a factory takes on the appearance of the goose that lays only golden eggs. There was an analogy in Bolivia. In 1952 the government nationalized the three big tin mines, with agreements to compensate; and since then have operated them through its agency, COMIBOL. Once COMIBOL took over, the people on the payrolls increased. This featherbedding, plus inefficient mining operations, made the cost of tin ore $1.40 a pound on the average, which is higher than the world price. A $40 million loan from the Inter-American Development Bank, West Germany, and the United States was promoted back in 1961 to deal with the tin mines. In 1963 COMIBOL began to press for technological reforms. This led to a strike and tremendous labor upheaval. Catawi, the center of this mining controversy, took on the name of Sierra Maestra, the name of Castro's old Cuban stronghold, and became the symbol of Bolivia's resistance. The Communist-coined object of the resistance was "Yankee imperialism," as it was the technical advice from the United States and the World Bank group that showed Bolivia how her tin mines could be modernized and made to pay.

The problems, of course, strike much deeper than this, and involve the education of managers and the training of technicians.

No matter what developing countries one visits, he is certain to find a very strong demand for trained businessmen. I have been associated with the Harvard Business School for some years in an advisory capacity, and on one of my recent overseas trips realized that if we took every single faculty member of the School and made him a Dean of a new Business School in some underdeveloped area, the need would still be far from satisfied.

The lack of technicians is notorious. Ten years ago when a municipal water system was being installed from artesian wells in Shiraz, Iran, it was discovered that there were no plumbers in the country. As a result, crews had to be sent to Europe for training.

In Guinea when independence came and Sekou Toure flouted the French, DeGaulle pulled out the French technicians and experts, leaving only a few trained Guineans. When I visited the country in 1965, the few engineers, scientists, and doctors that were available had all been drafted for municipal and national service in the bureaucracy that was needed to run the country. That meant that the only trained technicians that were available to administer to the needs of the people were engaged in other jobs, and if those needs were to be served experts would have to be brought in from the outside. So it was that Toure entered into technical assistance contracts with outside nations, mostly from eastern Europe. The winds of the Cold War were blowing so strong that Americans looked with askance upon the unorthodox system that Toure seemed to be developing.

The conditions vary country to country and continent to continent. In Latin America the educated man traditionally was learned in philosophy, law, and the arts, but very few in the sciences. The condition is illustrated in a painting I saw in a museum at Sucre, Bolivia. It epitomizes a saying of Flavius to the effect that while everyone wants virtue, few are willing to work for it. A Spaniard did this painting, which is dominated by four white horses, representing the only physical labor on the scene. Dozens of people stand idly around, each with his hands out. None turns a wheel; none cuts wood; none irrigates. No one does anything with his hands except to hold them out in supplication.

The message of the painting did not fully reach consciousness at the time. But that night at dinner with some of the university staff at Sucre, its message suddenly became clear. I had been saying — half in earnest, half in jest — that Bolivia is so far ahead of Africa in development (which is true) that Bolivia should have a Peace Corps there, showing Africans how to telescope several hundred years into a decade. To make my point, I said that if the first one hundred men and women around the world eminent in philosophy, law, sociology, anthropology, and the arts were listed, a goodly number would be Latin Americans.

My Bolivian friends agreed; but one went on to say:

> The riches of the mines ruined us Spaniards. With all the wealth pouring out of the earth, there was no reason to work with our hands. Let others do that. We would be the philosophers, the cultured people of the world. And we were. But look what happened! Look at Spain today! The Industrial Revolution for all practical purposes missed it. Look at Latin America! Engineering is for someone else. Mechanized farms are for other people. Industrial management? Buy the managers and bring them in to build and run our plants.

There was a long silence, for my friend spoke with sadness and his eyes were moist.

Holding out his hands he said, "We do not yet know how to work with them."

But that condition, though historically accurate, has radically changed. As for persons engaged in six principal professions in five Latin American nations, 1961-1965, the Pan American Health Organization gives the figures shown in the following table:

Professional group	Brazil	Chile	Argentina	Colombia	Ecuador
Physicians	....	5,200	35,400	7,500	2,500
Engineers	25,000	....	21,700	7,300	2,000
Lawyers	....	....	21,900	....	....
Dentists	....	3,300	14,100	2,500	....
Pharmacists ...	....	....	12,100	....	....
Architects	....	....	4,700	....	....

And the growth of graduate work in the sciences is shown by the table on p. 144.

Yet in spite of the awakening interest in science, the developing nations still have a non-scientific, if not an anti-scientific, attitude which bears heavily on their budgets and their high priority needs.

The need for trained personnel in developing countries is as great as the need for capital. Though there is capital pouring into a nation, it may go for naught unless there are technical, engineering, and managerial skills to put it to work. Secondly, while some developing

Country	Year	Humanities	Engineering	Natural sciences	Law	Medicine
Costa Rica	1960	6	21	5	24	20
Cuba	1962	66	70	23	83	458
Dominican Republic	1961	52	65	...	153	231
El Salvador	1959	...	20	15	14	33
Guatemala	1961	4	25	13	23	48
Haiti	1961	...	15	...	65	54
Honduras	1960	...	7	...	8	23
Jamaica	1960	56	...	33	...	31
Mexico	1960	12	818	239	558	1,341
Argentina	1962	1,566	1,167	497	1,432	4,363
Brazil	1961	3,302	1,489	784	3,509	3,989
Chile	1961	35	284	86	73	606
Colombia	1961	196	575	73	263	660
Ecuador	1961	2	36	1	89	288
Paraguay	1959	21	6	68	41	77
Peru	1959	7	204	297	389	810
Uruguay	1958	2	124	...	124	170
Venezuela	1961	144	312	31	385	831

nations have a large artisan class, the latter may be under pressures to leave the country. For example, East Africa is endowed with many Indians and Pakistanis who serve not only as merchants, bankers, and middlemen but also as artisans. The process of Africanization, however, is squeezing them out, even before Africans have acquired the necessary skills to take over. Hence the great urgency for the creation of technical and vocational schools.

ORT (Organization for Rehabilitation and Training located in Geneva and under Israeli auspices) has exciting technical training schools not only in Israel but in numerous developing nations. From my personal observations of ORT in Africa, I can say that while its cost is slight, its dividends are enormous.

Most of the industrialized nations have made some contribution to like training projects.

AID has numerous projects in developing countries for training drivers and mechanics, garment workers, typesetters, press operators, welders, electricians, woodworkers, cabinet makers, and for upgrading semi-skilled workers in various trades.

AID has several contracts with ORT (Kenya, Guinea, Gabon, and

Mali) for training artisans in various skills, e.g., auto maintenance, electricity, refrigeration, welding, carpentry, masonry, telecommunications, diesel engines, and the like.

The Sino-Soviet countries have carried on the largest technical assistance program outside the Western nations. It is estimated that they have supplied a total of at least 12,000 experts and technicians to the developing countries and at least 15,000 fellowships for training and education in Sino-Soviet countries, mostly in technical fields.

It is quite easy to take a boy from "the bush" in Africa and teach him how to assemble and repair radios. This is illustrative of part of the need. Beyond all that, however, is the development of a managerial elite — to establish an aristocracy of talent that will satisfy the needs for research and development, for planning, for efficient management of plants and public facilities, for propagation of the ideas of conservation. This is a staggering job for the developing nation; and no way has been found whereby it can be achieved in a hurry.

The Special Fund of the United Nations under Paul Hoffman had trained, as of June 30, 1967, 194,800 people for these tasks. The breakdown by regions is Africa: 33,200; the Americas: 73,300; Asia: 61,400; Europe: 15,700; Middle East: 11,200.

The breakdown by categories is: Technical Education (including university level engineering and agricultural, polytechnic and other): 63,600; Industrial Instructor Training: 51,800; Management and Supervisory Training: 46,600; Transport Training: 6,700; Communications Training: 10,900; Secondary School Teacher Training: 9,400; Public Administration and Economic Development Planning: 5,800.

In addition to these, there are about 180,000 men and women who have received some form of training under the Technical Assistance program.

A regional group known as the Asian Productivity Organization has been engaged in training people for the new responsibilities of the industrial age. This involves in part training in technological matters and also training in managerial skills. APO has been concentrating upon small industries which are not the typical village handicraft industries but shops and factories that are at least partly mechanized, are privately owned, and have tens of hundreds of workers. It has made numerous field studies. It has organized many seminars for the education of personnel and it has gone quite extensively into training of technical experts in such diverse fields as sugar, glass, soap, and textiles. Its trainees have added up to several thousand a year.

The need in developing nations for technical training has a high priority. In the first place many nations have few men and women skilled in automobile mechanics, let alone welding, masonry, radio repair, or even carpentry.

There are not many places, however, where one can get a technical or scientific training or a business school training in underdeveloped nations. The tragedy is that many who come here to this country or to Europe to study do not want to go back. They remember the miserable, stinking villages from which they came and the low standard of living that will face them on their return, and they are irresistibly drawn to the lush spots of the West.

Other reasons also influence that decision. The scientist trained in the West is often educated away from the problems of his own nation. His newly acquired education is more relevant, or seems to be more relevant, to problems here than to those at home. As Dr. Charles Frankel, until recently Assistant Secretary of State for Education and Cultural Affairs, pointed out, we "overtrain" some exchange visitors. For example, an Indian trained here as a high-energy physicist might not find a job back in India, but easily finds one in the United States, Great Britain, or Russia. Moreover, if his interest is in research and development, our laboratories and related facilities are more adequate for his needs than the ones he would find on his return, if there were any at all. These are not the only reasons why scientists and other professional people from underdeveloped nations seek careers here. But they are among the most important.

The result is commonly known as the "brain drain." It is one of the most ominous developments of the modern decade and one that will render largely futile attempts of developing nations to modernize agriculture and industry.

We start with the basic uncontestable fact that the United States, for various reasons, has a vast lead in science and technology over the western world and in applied science at least over the Soviet Union. The impact of this fact is felt not only in the developing world but also by some industrialized nations. The condition was forcefully stated on November 13, 1967, by Prime Minister Harold Wilson:

. . . there is no future for Europe, or for Britain, if we allow American business, and American industry so to dominate the strategic growth-industries of our individual countries, that they, and not we, are able to determine the pace and direction of Europe's industrial advance; then we are left in industrial terms as the hewers of wood and drawers of water while they, because of the scale of research, development and production which they can deploy, based on the vast size of their single market, come to enjoy a growing monopoly in the production of the technological instruments of industrial advance. As I said in Strasbourg, this is the road not to partnership but to an industrial helotry, which, as night follows day, will mean a declining influence in world affairs, for all of us in Europe.

We have to face this fact. One large American company today spends more on research and development every year than the annual trading turnover of the largest European company in the same field. In most of the industries which provide the mainspring of industrial advance in any nation, one American firm is equal in size, in profits, in cash-flow, to the whole industry in even our largest European states.

We have to face another fact too. Their advantage derives not only from the fact that the Americans have a wider and untrammelled Common Market. It is also because year by year the technological threshold gets higher so that no one in Europe can undertake the research, the development, and the financial risks of research and development on a continental scale unless they have a potential market going far beyond the limited 50 millions or so represented by the purchasing power of a single nation state in Europe.

We have to face a third fact, that while we in Britain have shown our determination to resist an American takeover of such vital industries as computers, and while we have a resolute, and aggressive civil nuclear industry, all of us in Europe are operating on too small a scale, and unless we can get on to a European scale, we face the danger of continuing penetration and takeover.

When it comes to the "brain drain," some European nations have drawn heavily on their neighbors. Sweden, for instance, attracts numerous Danish and Norwegian scientists. About 20 per cent of the Danish engineers work abroad, and one third of these have settled in Sweden.

Great Britain and France have attracted a large number of White Russians, Germans, and Austrians opposed to the Nazi regime, and Jews, from central and eastern Europe. These trends apparently have not stopped. In the last few years, West Germany has welcomed numerous scientists fleeing the Eastern Zone. At the present time, France accepts hundreds of Yugoslav and Polish architects who are in oversupply in their own countries.

Germany is a powerful magnet for German-speaking people from Switzerland and Austria. One-half of the Austrian university graduates are destined to move to Germany. Europe received, in return, one-third of the highly qualified German technicians who have emigrated in the last few years. In one specific case, the largest portion of the technicians who have left a German space-studies center in the last two and a half years (one-fourth of the total manpower) has moved to other European countries, especially France. The National Scientific Research Center of France employs 575 foreign scientists, most of whom are European and approximately 20 of whom are American.

Great Britain presents a different picture. She is situated at the crossroads of a "brain market" in which the participants are from the Commonwealth. Australia, New Zealand, South Africa, and Canada provide her with numerous highly qualified professionals. India and Pakistan also act as suppliers. England is the recipient of between one third and one half of all scientists emigrating from the Indian subcontinent. At the same time, Britain has lost through emigration a large percentage of her scientists who had acquired their doctorate, although only one half of them went to the United States.

The Freeman Report published by OECD in 1965 shows that, except for France and Italy, western Europe loses roughly 10 per cent of its native scientific and technical elite to the United States — a phenomenon which some call "a decimation of Europe." In the ten years that followed World War II, the stream of technically trained European immigrants to the United States increased sixfold, nearing 3,000 in 1957. The tide subsequently ebbed progressively to 1,600 in 1961. It has risen since then, there being about 2,500 engineers and scientists coming here from Europe in 1964.

Great Britain is the country which is most affected by the migration. England has more than twice as many emigrants as Germany, and more than ten times as many as France. An additional cause for worry in Britain is that, contrary to the trend in other countries, the rate of departures doubled from 1961 to 1964 (from 575 to 1,042).

In the case of Great Britain, the qualitative aspect of the outflow of scientists and technicians is particularly striking. Several official reports underline the fact that emigration has "created vacuums of serious consequence to the country's scientific development," and that many of the emigrating scientists are above average. The most recent case is that of Dr. Peter Murray, assistant director of Britain's atomic energy laboratory at Harwell, who was enticed away by Westinghouse.

In general, 5 per cent of America's scientists and technicians received their training in Europe, 17 per cent of the membership of the United States National Academy of Sciences were born or educated there, one fourth of America's Nobel Prize winners between 1907 and 1961 were of European origin, and six of Europe's laureates have since emigrated to the United States.

During the sixteen years from 1949 to 1964, 63,500 scientists and engineers, 85,000 if physicians are added, came to the United States from abroad, and settled permanently here.

The imported personnel (1962-1964) equaled 3 per cent the equivalent scientific personnel produced in the United States.

The current overall rate of 3 per cent represents the average of various rates for several categories which it encompasses: it is very low (.5 per cent) among social science graduates (economists and psychologists); is above 2 per cent for natural science graduates; and reaches 10 per cent for engineers. Over the last sixteen years the percentage of engineers fell from 75.2 per cent to 64.6 per cent of imported scientific personnel, in favor of professors and researchers. The inference is that there is a rise in the quality of immigrants.

The incoming scientists are not distributed equally among the various scientific and technical disciplines. Almost one half of the 10,600 engineers who immigrated between 1962 and 1964 entered the fields of electricity, mechanics, and public works. Concentration exists to an even greater extent in the sciences. The natural sciences have drained 4,600 scholars, 2,200 of whom were chemists, and 750 physicists.

The problem may get worse. While the federal government in 1940 spent only $74 million a year for research and development, that expenditure had risen to the billion dollar level in 1950 and reached $16 billion in 1967. Federal funds for research and development were then about 15 per cent of the federal budget. While a large portion went into national defense, almost half reached strictly nonmilitary areas. This federal money finances about three-quarters of all our scientific research. Moreover, it is federal money that supports the most advanced research.

Many scientists feel that continuing federal support for science and technology on the present scale is irreversible for various practical reasons. On that premise the technological advance in the last third of this century may dwarf even the startling advances of the last thirty years.

The cost of our war in Vietnam — $2.5 billion a month — is beginning to discount that prediction, for research and development funds have been decreasing in recent months. Yet barring catastrophic circumstances, the American scientific lead will doubtless be maintained.

This American invasion of the Continent is serious and alarming to many European countries. The Japanese are also concerned. A survey indicates that more than 1 out of 10 university graduates and young professionals want to live abroad. Moreover, overall emigration from Japan — particularly to the United States and Canada — picked up in 1966 after a seven-year period of decline. Japan, though not a developing nation, probably can ill-afford to lose even a small number of its scientific elite. The problem at the level of the industrialized countries, however, does not compare in gravity with the "brain drain" being suffered by the developing countries.

There are no complete figures that show the entire picture of the "brain drain" from developing nations to this country. The best sources are the 1966 report of the Pan American Health Organization, Reports of the National Science Foundation, and a 1967 Staff Study for the House Committee on Government Operations. Immigration statistics alone are not reliable, as scientists are often only tourists or here on short professional engagements. Countries from which a person comes may conceal an immigration from a developing nation. For a developed nation may be merely a way station for a scientist en route from India or some other developing nation to the United States. Some figures are of necessity only estimates. But the dimensions of the problem, though seen darkly in the various studies, are sufficiently clear to give us a measure of its threat to the developing nations.

When we turn to the developing countries, it is obvious that the movement of the specialists is not entirely one way. Kerala, one of India's southern states, has doctors here and in Great Britain. Great Britain has physicians here and in India. We too have doctors in India. When this kind of movement is plotted, it is seen that the widening of the gap is being slowed down. Yet the developing nations make a much greater contribution to the mature ones than the latter to the former.

Some say that the total scientific brain drain into the United States is not important. They point to the fact that scientists who are immigrants are only a small percentage of United States graduates in science, ranging from 2.2 per cent in 1956 to 1.9 per cent in 1966.

But for the engineers, the percentages are much higher — 8.9 per cent in 1956 and 9.5 per cent in 1966.

And the figures for physicians are even higher — 15.7 per cent in 1956 and 26.1 per cent in 1966.

Whatever impact this trained personnel may have here, the measure of the problem is in the weakening of the professional ranks available to the developing nations from which they came.

Some of the experts think that even Britain is disadvantaged, not by inferior brains, but by a productivity system that is geared less to technology than to manual workers, who in turn are slowed up by poor plants. Moreover, when England recently tried to reclaim some of her physicians from this country, it appeared that they would not have left home and would willingly return, if the cumbersome machinery of British medicare were renovated so as to allow a physician a chance for an easier escalation up the professional ladder. In that particular spot of the spectrum, England then would be in the same posture as a developing nation.

Great Britain has 4,000 foreign physicians; we have 20,000; and our hospitals have 11,000 interns and residents with foreign diplomas — an amount that is 27 per cent of the active hospital staff. A salary of about $500, with free room and board, constitutes a financial reward which they could not hope for in their own country. But the attraction of American hospitals is more than financial. Numerous physicians choose to work in the United States in order to join brilliant medical research teams endowed with the priceless benefits of freedom of thought and unlimited material means. Many doctors who came to the United States for specialized additional training were seduced by fringe benefits and stayed here.

We turn out 8,000 physicians a year, though 12,000 are needed, due largely to the Malthusian policy of the American Medical Association. Each year we authorize 1,400 foreign-trained physicians and surgeons (about 400 being American) to practice here. In 1963 there were 16 Nigerian doctors working here. While we have one doctor for every 600 people, Nigeria has only one doctor per 50,000 people. Some say there are more Iranian doctors here than in Iran, which is likewise short of doctors. India has 1,500 doctors here; there are several hundred Israelis; 500 Turks; 300 Dominicans; about 5,000 from all of Latin America. If the cost of training a physician is set at $60,000, it is clear that the developing nations, when they send us 20,000 doctors, are giving us aid of $1.2 billion.

We have now 100,000 foreign students a year, as compared to 65,000 five years ago. About one ninth of the total express the wish to remain here; about 30 per cent of those who come from Asian countries are included in that one ninth.

In the last three years Asia has contributed about 3,000 people to our scientific and technical wealth. At the end of 1966 it was estimated that 1,143 Indians taught in American universities and colleges. At the same time, only 92 Americans filled similar positions in India. This represents a disequilibrium ratio of 10 to .8. In 1965, 574 Latin American engineers settled in the United States. The New York Office of the Israeli Ministry of Labor estimates that there are in the United States several hundred graduate engineers from the Polytechnical School of Haifa and a high number of young graduates of Hebrew University, including eminent physicists and mathematicians, now very much in demand. Some of these scholars are not necessarily "lost" to Israel since many express the desire to return "sooner or later." Countries as manifestly underdeveloped as Kenya, Egypt, Algeria, Tunisia, Morocco, Korea, and Thailand witness the emigration to the United States of some of their rare specialists.

These figures from developing nations are only approximate, for, as noted, reliable statistics are not kept. Moreover, numbers alone are not a measure of the problem, for one person with the extraordinary gift of leadership would be uniquely valuable in his own nation, worth perhaps 100 other well-trained professionals.

Further, one developing nation may have a smaller base of professional people than another. For example, Colombia has 50 physicians for every 10,000 people while Argentina has about 150. Colombia has 7,000 engineers; Argentina, 22,000. In general, Argentina has a skilled professional manpower base about three times as large as Colombia's. Thus the loss of a single person is about three times more serious to Colombia than to Argentina.

The Pan American Health Organization, speaking for Latin America, concludes that on the whole the losses due to the "brain drain" are more serious in medicine and science than in engineering. For the demand for locally trained engineers is typically high in Latin America and the salaries are relatively fixed. Moreover, relatively few engineers speak English.

As for doctors, about 300 migrate from Latin America to the United States annually, a number that is equal to the annual output of three large United States medical schools. If the cost of building three schools and the annual cost of operating them are added, PAHO estimates that the value of physicians coming to the United States is roughly equal to that of all medical assistance given by the United States to Latin America.

Three out of four migrating doctors come from Argentina, Colombia, Mexico, and Peru.

About 575 engineers from Latin America were admitted to the United States with immigrant visas in 1965. Although the exact number of permanent immigrants is not known, PAHO notes that the figures on engineer migrants tend to be high.

Only 13 mathematicians and physicists came here from Latin America (Cuba excluded) in that year.

From 1960 to 1965 about 3,000 permanent migrants of all professional people came here from Latin America.

While engineers in Latin America are ready to begin their careers on graduation, a scientist requires further training, which often can be received only abroad. Moreover, scientists, more than engineers, tend to be members of an international community. People working on the same problem are scattered throughout the world. A scientist can become mobile without seriously disrupting his work, and his opportunities are not as bright at home as in the laboratories of the United States. There does not, however, seem to be a high migration of scientists from Latin America, the main reason being that few scientists exist there. But the migration of the few means the tragic loss of a significant portion of the total number in each developing country.

In the years 1956 and 1962-1966, the number of scientists, engineers, and physicians migrating here from developing countries was generally on the increase.

Fiscal Year	Number	Per Cent of Total
1956	1769	32.9
1962	2383	40.0
1963	3362	42.6
1964	3203	41.0
1965	2650	36.8
1966	4390	46.0

These figures probably substantially understate the actual contribution of the developing countries since Canada, a developed nation, is a notorious way station for many who ultimately come here.

Of the 15,992 engineers and scientists who came here in 1962-1964, 8,415 came from Europe and 1,844 from Canada. Mexico and South America contributed 1,046 (not including Cuba) and 2,597 came from Asia.

In 1966 scientists, engineers, and physicians arriving here from Asia numbered 2,736; those from South America 807; and those from Africa, 129.

Of the 4,259 scientists registered here in 1964 as holders of foreign doctorates, there were 422 from Asia; 3 from Mexico; 49 from South America; 22 from Africa.

Of the 918 scientists registered here in 1964 as holders of foreign master's degrees, there were 214 from Asia; 8 from Mexico; 8 from South America; 20 from Africa.

(The holders of doctorates and masters are approximate only as the registration was voluntary.)

The impact of the "brain drain" on developing nations is emphasized by the fact that of all scientists, engineers, and physicians who immigrate here, the percentage who come from developing nations was 32.9 per cent in 1956, and 46.0 per cent in 1966.

There is, of course, a net gain to a developing country whose professionals emigrate here to the extent that its students in science who come here for degrees return home. But it is estimated that the actual net gain after immigration losses are taken into account is only three out of ten new graduates.

The number of qualified professional people waiting abroad for immigration visas but who could not be accommodated rose from 3,000 in 1966 to 8,400 in 1967. The former will be reflected in the immigration figures for 1967, the latter in those for 1968.

Under our Immigration Law, an exchange visitor is required to return home or go to another cooperating country for two years before he can apply for immigration. But the Act provides that the Attorney General may waive this foreign residence requirement "in the public interest" on the request of an interested federal agency and the recommendation of the Secretary of State. Four federal agencies, including AEC, use this waiver provision to keep highly qualified foreign scientists here. HEW and NASA are among the four. The practice is so common that the four agencies have standardized forms to speed up the program. In 1966 waivers were granted in 290 cases so that professional people from abroad could work here. All but 80 were from developing nations.

Under our 1965 immigration law, nonwestern hemisphere countries from 1969 onwards will be limited to a global total of 170,000 immigration visas. Of these, 17,000 are available to immigrants "who are members of the professions, or who because of their exceptional ability in the sciences or arts will substantially benefit projectively the national economy, cultural interests, or welfare of the United States", 79 Stat. 913. Even if half of that 17,000 is absorbed by dependents, the other half can qualify under another quota of 17,000 described as immigrants "capable of performing specified skilled or unskilled labor, not of a temporary or seasonal nature, for which a shortage of employable and willing persons exists in the United States" 79 Stat. 913. So Asia that sent us 2,736 scientists, engineers, and physicians in 1966 may send us several times that during each year in the days ahead. And the worldwide number of 9,068 in 1966 (exclusive of South America) can nearly double.

As already indicated, the emigration of Japanese scientists started to pick up in 1966; and it is confidently expected that the new immigration law will increase the rate and number.

So the problem promises to get more, rather than less, acute.

What to do about the problem is the difficult question.

When scientists in developing countries are so discouraged by obstacles to a career in science and teaching at home that they migrate, they are in effect *pushed* out of their countries. Dr. Atma Ram, Director General of India's Council of Scientific and Industrial research, observed recently that the real solution for enticing native specialists back from foreign countries lies in the economic growth of the home country. The creation of the necessary climate in the home country as well as the research facilities and laboratories adequate for modern scientific projects is, however, a long-range problem. It is indeed as distant and remote as supplanting an archaic agricultural society with an industrial complex that has its own vigorous projects of research and development competing with our own.

Making the United States unattractive to scientists also presupposes a hypothetical train of events that we cannot predict or control.

So we face a situation where the *push* out of a developing country and the *pull* toward this nation will remain relatively constant.

The chances for influencing either one of these forces concerns only the *rate* of immigration, not complete *stoppage*. Closing the doors here would indeed be unwise. For the community of scientific scholars is a close one; communications between them is important; their real education is in the classroom and laboratories of the world.

Iqbal, the Moslem poet from Lahore, said that the great contribution of the West to the East was the scientific attitude, the great contribution of the East being charity or love, as epitomized by Christ and Mohammed, Confucius and Buddha.

> In the West, intellect is the source of life
> In the East, Love is the basis of life.
> Through Love, Intellect grows acquainted with Reality,
> and Intellect gives stability to the work of Love,
> Arise and lay the foundations of a new world,
> By wedding Intellect to Love.

This is the unfinished business which the brain drain from developing nations is retarding.

At a hearing on the brain drain conducted by a subcommittee of the House Committee on Government Operations in January, 1968, it was revealed that between 1966 and 1967 the brain drain to the United States from less developed countries increased at a faster rate than that from developed countries.

Scientific immigration from the former nations now represents more than half of the total. More than 40 per cent of this immigration from developing countries is attributable to student nonreturn, as compared with 4 per cent student nonreturn for the developed countries.

Bringing foreign students from developing nations here on grants from their own governments, promises some relief. Statistics show that those who come here under those auspices usually return, less than 1 per cent staying. There is, first, the feeling of moral obligation to return; and second, when a foreign nation prescribes education abroad, it is usually designed in light of the requirements for employment at home in a preselected field. Conceivably then a developing country could determine its high-priority needs, create the positions to be filled by trainees going to the United States, and make as certain as possible that the education received here would relate to their future tasks back home.

What I have proposed is not particularly relevant to the need for engineers or for physicians in the rural areas of Latin America, Asia, or the Middle East. Scientists are in a real sense the key.

What is relevant to the problem of the scientists is the creation in the developing nations of the economic, political, social, and technological conditions that will make their homeland more attractive than the United States. This was perhaps the main recommendation coming out of the Lausanne, Switzerland, Brain Drain Conference of August, 1967. The place to start is with the scientist, for he is small in number and the total investment needed for him and his research-and-development facilities is less than the overall technological need. The governments of developing nations generally have an anti-scientific attitude or at least a non-scientific attitude. That must be changed and scientific centers established in these nations. Agencies of the UN can be helpful. Private foundations can help. Where one developing nation has creditable facilities in a particular field, even American scholarship aid can be given to students from developing nations studying there, rather than here. That has indeed been one of the projects of AID.

AID has also supported quality institutions for research and teaching in the developing countries. One example is the Korean Institute of Science and Technology. Moreover, AID is assisting some countries in establishing national research councils and in devising science policies.

Our Cal Tech's and MIT's can help establish satellites, not to feed our industrial complex, but to serve the needs of developing nations in some appropriate regional grouping.

At the business or managerial level, the Harvard Business School has made numerous contributions, mainly by sending faculty members abroad to teach in existing schools for a year or so. In Central America it fathered the Institute of Management in Central America (INCAE), which was financed in part by AID and in part by regional businessmen and which is located at Managua, Nicaragua.

But what has been done to establish abroad technical and scientific institutes or business and management institutes is miniscule. What has been done is a mere token of what must be done to satisfy the unquenched thirst for education of a scientific and a business elite.

PAHO has recommended that each developing nation have a repatriation program that has both a statistical and an action aspect. There are few reliable statistical data for any one country. A nation that kept track of its emigrees could keep track of those who are highly trained and stay abroad. They could then make attractive tenders for their return, e.g., housing accommodations at reasonable prices, tax-exempt privileges on the importation of household goods, an automobile, assured support for research, and assured career opportunities. Moreover, wherever the idea is palatable in a political sense, we, the developed nations, can send trained persons to the developing nations — to be teachers, to head research centers, to train local cadres.

We can make our immigration laws congenial to the foreign student but less cordial to the professional man or woman who, having been trained here or in Europe, seeks his career in this country. Modification of these laws may in time turn out to be as important in terms of foreign aid as capital grants or loans.

Technical assistance is probably much more important than capital assistance, though the two go hand in hand.

We can take a chapter from the Soviets' book when it comes to such aid. I saw it in operation in Outer Mongolia and it worked well. Russia makes loans, not grants; and the loans carry 2.5 per cent interest. When I was there, a leather factory was being built with a Russian loan under the supervision of Russian engineers. When the construction work started, the Mongolian staff that would run the factory had been shipped off to Russia to learn the secrets of the management of that factory. They would work in a leather factory in Russia and return to Mongolia in six months or a year. These technical skills can be easily transmitted. Managerial skills come more slowly. Yet personnel training can take place fairly rapidly.

We could do a like job in Latin America if we chose to be adventuresome. Our loan would be to a public entity which, as noted, the World Bank Group frequently finances. We could train here in a like facility the entire personnel that would man the Latin American factory.

This requires planning and promotion and the discreet choice of key industries to finance. But this system could transform the face of the key areas in Latin America. At the present juncture the great demanding need is for that kind of technical assistance that not only produces the artisans and the men who can man the new factory that is built, but also the managerial group that is strong in research, strong in analysis, strong in development, and strong in problem-solving competence.

On my foreign travels I ended with a sense of sadness,

— sadness at the sight of the abysmal poverty and illiteracy that possess the people at the bottom;

— sadness at the graft and corruption at the top;

— sadness at the powerful attraction that the United States and Europe has for the trained men and women who should stay at home making bricks with such straw as they can find.

Western culture has in a sense captured the world and the standard of living in an affluent society is so high and the First Amendment freedoms are so vivid in the lives of the people that all who can arrange it want to come here. It is a sort of a strange, symbiotic relationship that can have destructive as well as sustaining features. I remember the *palo santo* tree that I saw in the jungles of Latin America. The tree has such a reddish hue that it is instantly identified. It is distinguished for its symbiotic relation with ants. Colonies of ants possess it, eating the nectar of its flowers and the sap that flows from it. In return, the ants protect the tree from all intruders. If a vine or the branch of another tree touches a *palo santo,* the ants move into action and utterly destroy the invader. Should an animal start up the tree, they devour it. A member of our Peace Corps, in stringing a hammock, innocently tied a rope to a *palo santo* tree and could hardly get the rope untied, the onset of ants was so ferocious. In 1962, a *campesino,* learning that his wife had been unfaithful, tied her to a *palo santo* tree and in a short time the ants ate her up down to her bones.

We of the West are not necessarily destined to be the world's *palo santo* tree. One alternative is a reverse flow of technical skills, filling the developing nations with their own scientistsandengineers.The problem is universal in scope. M. D. Millionshchikov, Vice President of the Academy of Sciences, USSR, told me:

> In the Soviet Union we have raised the national economies, as well as the cultural and scientific levels, of our national republics. The basic principle we followed was that it is necessary to create in the country itself its own intellectual and professional cadre, its own engineers and technicians, its own scientists and scientific institutions, its own institutions for the training of a hard core of personnel who would have outside help, to be sure, but from sources experienced in specific fields, not just generalized "aid."

Discovery or invention of the devices that will make this trend possible implicates all international agencies. The industrial nations, including of course Russia, must design cooperative projects that will bring the reverse trend off.

The differences between "capitalism" and "communism" grow more and more indistinct. The market economy that once meant "capitalism," and control planning that once meant "communism," have become blended. Differences remain; but they are not so much ideological as managerial and technical.

Only those whose thinking firmly jelled a quarter of a century ago can persist in pursuit of the Cold War. The masters of technology on both sides of the old Iron Curtain have new and common responsibilities. They must become collaborators in designing technological blueprints for the developing nations.

There are those who think that even if the rich nations invested 1 per cent of their GNP in the developing nations, the rate of development would not be substantially accelerated. The reason is that while it is easy to take a man from the bush in Africa, for example, and train him to work at a lathe, it is very difficult to develop a precise blueprint of what a particular nation may need in terms of technical or managerial skills. In other words, our ignorance concerning the needs of the developing countries is rather substantial.

Even though technical training matches the needs of a developing country, there simply are not enough people in those countries to make the difficult decisions respecting development and to solve the many complex problems involved in it. What is needed goes far beyond trained technicians such as plumbers, radio repairmen, welders, masons, and the like. What is needed is an elite of trained manpower capable of making plans, of solving problems, of making decisions, and a time scale for training people. This means decades rather than years. These plans must be designed for the long range — a minimum perhaps of fifty years. As Harrison-Brown has stated, the "time scale for development must be the time scale for training people."

If we are to get on with this, I think the elite of our professional people must spend most of their lives in teaching and heading research in the developing countries. It means the establishment in the developing countries of institutions which will in time turn out the elite necessary to manage the new industrial regimes that will be born. This requires bi-lateral undertakings of vast magnitude. It means that the donor countries must come from all industrialized nations, including the Communist group. Even if we and Europe and the Soviet Union made available a certain percentage of our trained engineers, scientists, teachers, and professors to work, teach, and do research in these developing countries, decades would be involved.

Happily our scientists and the scientists from the Communist world have had both experience and success in working across national boundaries on problems of mutual concern. The pooling of these technical resources, perhaps through the United Nations, would make a challenging start on problems that today seem so difficult as to be almost beyond reach.

We face the enormous task of regional and international planning that takes account of human needs, financial resources, and scientific manpower. The place to start is with Paul Hoffman's Special Fund of the UN and the new UN agency, United Nations Industrial Development Organization (UNIDO), which so far has been mainly engaged in overcoming production and managerial bottlenecks in developing nations.

Whether we start with human needs, with foreign aid, or with the "brain drain," our problem is the creation of programs of international cooperation which will treat the developing nations at this point in history as a responsibility of the international community.

Chapter V

The Crippling Effects
of Ideology and Racism

Like the giant Brobdingnagian in *Gulliver's Travels,* America is being threatened with impotence by pygmies.

One group of pygmies carries the banner of the Cold War; the other flies the flag of racism.

The Cold War has made us largely impotent abroad. The "enemy" is Moscow, or Peking, or Warsaw, or Hanoi today. The "enemy" may indeed by any Communist Country, whether it be prosperous Outer Mongolia, progressive Yugoslavia, impoverished Vietnam, or nearby Cuba.

The Cold War was the creation of Stalin, Truman, and Churchill. It was based on the theory that communism was not only evil but expansionist, not only ravenous but guided and controlled by some evil genie that would one day consume the world.

The cause of the Cold War was served by an armament race which has come to give us an overwhelming commitment to military might and a military mentality.

The cause of the Cold War was served in this country by a "witch hunt." The late Joe McCarthy gave impetus to that "witch hunt" from his seat in the Senate. But Truman — and later Eisenhower — gave it new wings through the Loyalty and Security programs whereby we put on a massive search for every ideological stray. The pattern was as follows:

Q. Do you believe in socialized medicine?
A. Yes.
Q. Should Peking be admitted to the United Nations?
A. Yes.

And so the questioning continued in an effort to produce "parallelism" in thought between the employee on the government payroll and Communist ideology. Parallelism was usually enough to cast the employee into the outer darkness, making him ineligible from then on for government employment.

Millions of employees of government agencies and of government contractors were put through this process. The impact was measurable not only by the number of people discharged but by the blanket of fear and nervous caution that was cast over the entire populace. As a result of these loyalty-security hearings and of the investigations by legislative committees into people's beliefs and opinions, we all became hesitant to espouse the off-beat, unorthodox idea. We all became more and more conformist.

Teachers were plagued with loyalty oaths that made it hazardous for them to have any association even with international scientific groups containing a sizeable Communist element. Many were discharged for promoting racial desegregation. They were often put to the test of defending their attitudes towards unpopular ideas such as "socialism." Moreover, the vast expenditures of public funds, much of it from the Pentagon, to finance research has had a limiting effect on our thinking. The spectrum of ideas, open at colleges and universities, has been perceptibly narrowed. While the reasons have varied, our educational institutions have ceased to be great centers of change and revolution; they had indeed become more and more spokesmen for the *status quo*. Their promotion of diversity as an active, powerful force in our lives has largely ceased.

Other forces have contributed to our trend toward conformity.

A sure-fire way for a person to campaign for public office has been as simply "anti-Communist." A sure-fire way to defeat almost anyone has been to tag him a "Communist."

The news poured out by the mass media has been highly colored. Subtle suggestions of "Communist" plots, intimations that a subversive thought was behind a particular pronouncement, a constant hammering away at communism became characteristics of our press, radio, and TV. Those who lived here all the time became used to it; but it always was a shock to those of us who traveled the back reaches of the world to hear it, see it, and read it when we returned after a long absence.

The American mind got so conditioned to "anti-communism" that we become paranoid. There was, we thought, a great conspiracy against us. So most collaborative efforts with the Communist bloc became useless or futile.

This meant that we relied more and more on military strategy and tactics, less and less on cooperative undertakings.

Our presence in Vietnam was from the start a sad mark of our political bankruptcy to deal with world problems under a regime of diplomacy and law.

There is of course such a thing as communism and it does use espionage, as do others; but communism is not monolithic. Peking is on the extreme left; Moscow is in the middle; Yugoslavia, Outer Mongolia, Poland, Czechoslovakia, Roumania and Vietnam are on the right. And Vietnam's greatest fear is actually not the United States but Peking.

The driving forces at the world level are Nationalism, Race, and Poverty. Sometimes they put on a Communist garb. But the Poor, the Communists, the Browns, Yellows, and Blacks are not our implacable enemies. There are common denominators for all people the world around.

While the Cold War was largely responsible for our Vietnam venture, there was, as well, another powerful subconscious influence operating insidiously. For our domestic political philosophy has long rested on an unstated premise of white supremacy.

The Negro escaped slavery but he did not escape the badges of slavery. Slavery meant inferiority as well as servitude. The Black Codes represented a way of life that was approved between 1868, when the Fourteenth Amendment was adopted, and 1954, when the Court held segregation of the races in public facilities unconstitutional. "Separate but equal" was one badge of slavery or inferiority. The disqualification of Negroes to be members of many trade unions was another. The examples are legion. The Negro was not the sole victim of discrimination. Americans of Mexican ancestry were put in segregated schools in southwest border states. Chinese were not admitted to white schools in Mississippi.

Los Angeles still has segregated schools in three categories:

   76 segregated schools for Americans of
  104 segregated schools for Americans of
       African ancestry
       Mexican ancestry
  355 predominantly white schools

These are not completely segregated schools; but about half of the Americans of Mexican ancestry are in their segregated schools; about nine-tenths of the Americans of African ancestry are in their segregated schools, and about 96 per cent of the whites are in their segregated schools.

The median figures are more telling:

In the Mexican American schools the median has a ratio of about ten Mexican Americans to one white.

In the Negro schools the median has a ratio of more than a hundred Negroes to one white.

In the white schools the median has a ratio of six to eight hundred whites to one Negro.

In other ways we have created systems of discrimination (albeit subtle ones) against Americans of Chinese and Japanese ancestry, as well as the American Indian.

The legal battle for civil rights was finally won almost a hundred years after the adoption of the Fourteenth Amendment in 1868. But to many that victory seemed largely empty without realization of equality of economic opportunities; and those opportunities were not always forthcoming.

When the whites of eastern Europe opted for communism (or were forced into it), we did not send expeditionary forces to oppose them. But the colored people of Asia fare differently. The Yellow Peril is an old slogan that our press has exploited. Discrimination against the Chinese and Japanese has long been a force in our lives as evidenced by a persistent pattern of state laws.

Martin Luther King, Jr. was quite right in relating Vietnam to many of the problems of our urban ghettos. No slogan of the Brown Peril has been coined; and it is probably below the level of the conscious mind. But it is there in close association with a mindfulness of the Yellow Peril. Indeed many think of our struggle in Vietnam as a war that somehow or other will contain China.

When we finally grant full equality to all races at home, we will have rejoined the human race. Then all problems — domestic and international — will be manageable. Until we rejoin the human race, we will be largely impotent to cope with any problem, Communist or not, that has a racial overtone.

A multi-religious, multi-racial, multi-ideological community is our constitutional ideal. We have made great progress in keeping Church and State separate, allowing no sect to obtain governmental preference or support and allowing the concept of religious liberty to enjoy a full flowering.

We have not made the same progress when it comes to race even though our Constitution is color blind.

Though the First Amendment makes a man's beliefs his own business, we have let them become too much and too often the concern of Big Brother. Yet as Jefferson said, government has no rightful concern with what people think or believe unless and until their thoughts become translated into action.

Nonetheless the pygmies of prejudice still continue to possess us when it comes to Race and Ideology.

These handicaps which possess us can be removed only by our unilateral action. Their removal, however, would not solve our world problems. A consensus with other nations is needed; and a consensus by definition cannot be imposed by one nation's *fiat*.

Some will argue that the removal of these handicaps will not make a whit of difference, because the forces loose in the world are unmanageable and beyond the reach of Reason which a Dialogue could enlighten. These pessimists may be right. But if so, we march to Armaggedon without remedy or recourse.

Yet we owe ourselves, as well as posterity, an effort in the other direction. We can, I think, become a powerful moral force in helping design a Rule of Law to govern the troublesome problems of the world, if we rid ourselves of the pygmies that have made Ideology and Race crippling forces in our lives and attitudes.

Those two forces have made us all — East and West — react to racial and ideological, rather than to human problems. The bourgeois capitalist has become the image of the enemy to millions. The Communist has become the image of the enemy to the others. The Yellow Peril becomes an obsession. Yet humanity, not ideology, is our common concern. That means that the main problem of the oncoming generation is to find practical ways of making a viable world out of that common concern.

That means removing the barriers of travel and lifting all taboos on conversation and debate. It means bringing all nations into the United Nations. It means free association with all the nonconformists of the world to see if somehow common denominators can be found so that the Rich and the Poor, White and Colored, can deal with these four central problems of the international community as they are presented late in the twentieth century.

Index

About the Author

WILLIAM ORVILLE DOUGLAS was born in Maine, Minnesota, the son of a Home Missionary of the Presbyterian Church. He attended grade school and high school in Yakima, Washington, received his AB from Whitman College, Walla Walla, and his LLD from Columbia Law School in New York. He was a member of the Columbia and Yale law faculties and served in a legal capacity on a number of government commissions. He was nominated by President Roosevelt to be an Associate Justice of the Supreme Court, and took his seat on April 17, 1939.

Justice Douglas has written many books both on jurisprudence and on his other great interests, travel and conservation. Among the best known are *Of Men and Mountains, Beyond the High Himalayas, An Almanac of Liberty, Russian Journey,* and *A Wilderness Bill of Rights.*

3 5282 00310 1725